Third Edition

Bicycle
Trails
of
Minnesota

An
American Bike Trails
Publication

Third Edition
Bicycle Trails of **Minnesota**

Published by American Bike Trails

Created by   Ray Hoven

Illustrated & Designed by   Mary C. Rumpsa

Table of Contents

Table of Contents (continued)

How To Use This Book

This book provides a comprehensive, easy-to-use quick reference to the many off-road trails throughout Minnesota. It includes details on over 100 trails and 75 detailed trail maps, plus overviews covering the state by section, organized by south, north and the Twin Cities metro area. Trails are generally listed alphabetically within each section. Sectional overviews preside each section, with a cross-reference by city and by county in the back. Each trail map includes such helpful features as location and access, trail facilities, and nearby communities.

Terms Used

Length	Expressed in miles one way. Round trip mileage is normally indicated for loops.	
Effort Levels	**Easy**	Physical exertion is not strenuous. Climbs and descents as well as technical obstacles are more minimal. Recommended for beginners.
	Moderate	Physical exertion is not excessive. Climbs and descents can be challenging. Expect some technical obstacles.
	Difficult	Physical exertion is demanding. Climbs and descents require good riding skills. Trail surface may be sandy, loose rock, soft or wet.
Directions	Describes by way of directions and distances, how to get to the trail areas from roads and nearby communities.	
Map	Illustrative representation of a geographic area, such as a state, section, forest, park or trail complex.	
DNR	Department of Natural Resources	
DOT	Department of Transportation	

Types of Biking

Mountain	Fat-tired bikes are recommended. Ride may be generally flat but then with a soft, rocky or wet surface.
Leisure	Off-road gentle ride. Surface is generally paved or screened.
Tour	Riding on roads with motorized traffic or on road shoulders.

Riding Tips

- Pushing in gears that are too high can push knees beyond their limits. Avoid extremes by pedaling faster rather than shifting into a higher gear.

- Keeping your elbows bent, changing your hand position frequently and wearing bicycle gloves all help to reduce the numbness or pain in the palm of the hand from long-distance riding.

- Keep you pedal rpms up on an uphill so you have reserve power if you lose speed.

- Stay in a high-gear on a level surface, placing pressure on the pedals and resting on the handle bars and saddle.

- Lower your center of gravity on a long or steep downhill run by using the quick release seat post binder and dropping the saddle height down.

- Brake intermittently on a rough surface.

- Wear proper equipment. Wear a helmet that is approved by the Snell Memorial Foundation or the American National Standards Institute. Look for one of their stickers inside the helmet.

- Use a lower tire inflation pressure for riding on unpaved surfaces. The lower pressure will provide better tire traction and a more comfortable ride.

- Apply your brakes gradually to maintain control on loose gravel or soil.

- Ride only on trails designated for bicycles or in areas where you have the permission of the landowner.

- Be courteous to hikers or horseback riders on the trail, they have the right of way.

- Leave riding trails in the condition you found them. Be sensitive to the environment. Properly dispose of your trash. If you open a gate, close it behind you.

- Don't carry items or attach anything to your bicycle that might hinder your vision or control.

- Don't wear anything that restricts your hearing.

- Don't carry extra clothing where it can hang down and jam in a wheel.

Explanation of Symbols

SYMBOL LEGEND	
🏊	Beach/Swimming
🚲	Bicycle Repair
🏚	Cabin
⛺	Camping
🛶	Canoe Launch
✚	First Aid
🍴	Food
GC	Golf Course
?	Information
🛏	Lodging
MF	Multi-Facilities
P	Parking
🛆	Picnic
🚶	Ranger Station
🚹🚺	Restrooms
🏠	Shelter
T	Trailhead
🏛	Visitor Center
🚰	Water
🔭	Overlook/ Observation

AREA LEGEND	
▨	City, Town
▨	Parks, Preserves
▢	Waterway
▨	Marsh/Wetland
▬▬	Mileage Scale
★	Points of Interest
– –	County/State
🌲	Forest/Woods

TRAIL LEGEND	
▬▬▬▬	Bike Trail
▭▭▭▭	Bicycle Lanes
··············	Hiking only Trail
●●●●●●●●	Multi Use Trail
▬▬▬▬	Snowmobiling only
= = = = = =	Planned Trail
▬ ▬ ▬ ▬	Alternate Trail
▬▬▬▬	Road/Highway
++++++++++	Railroad Tracks

Health Hazards

Hypothermia

Hypothermia is a condition where the core body temperature falls below 90 degrees. This may cause death.

Mild hypothermia

1. Symptoms
   a. Pronounced shivering
   b. Loss of physical coordination
   c. Thinking becomes cloudy
2. Causes
   a. Cold, wet, loss of body heat, wind
3. Treatment
   a. Prevent further heat loss, get out of wet clothing and out of wind. Replace wet clothing with dry.
   b. Help body generate more heat. Refuel with high-energy foods and a hot drink, get moving around, light exercise, or external heat.

Severe hypothermia

1. Symptoms
   a. Shivering stops, pulse and respiration slows down, speech becomes incoherent.
2. Treatment
   a. Get help immediately.
   b. Don't give food or water.
   c. Don't try to rewarm the victim in the field.
   d. A buildup of toxic wastes and tactic acid accumulates in the blood in the body's extremities. Movement or rough handling will cause a flow of the blood from the extremities to the heart. This polluted blood can send the heart into ventricular fibrillations (heart attack). This may result in death.
   e. Wrap victim in several sleeping bags and insulate from the ground.

Frostbite

Symptoms of frostbite may include red skin with white blotches due to lack of circulation. Rewarm body part gently. Do not immerse in hot water or rub to restore circulation, as both will destroy skin cells.

Heat Exhaustion

Cool, pale, and moist skin, heavy sweating, headache, nausea, dizziness and vomiting. Body temperature nearly normal.

Treatment: Have victim lie in the coolest place available – on back with feet raised. Rub body gently with cool, wet cloth. Give person glass of water every 15 minutes if conscious and can tolerate it. Call for emergency medical assistance.

Heat Stroke

Hot, red skin, shock or unconsciousness; high body temperature.

Treatment: Treat as a life-threatening emergency. Call for emergency medical assistance immediately. Cool victim by any means possible. Cool bath, pour cool water over body, or wrap wet sheets around body. Give nothing by mouth.

Explanation of Geographical Terms

Bog	An acidic wetland that is fed by rainwater and is characterized by open water with a floating mat of vegetation (e.g. sedges, mosses, tamarack) that will often bounce if you jump on it.
Bluff	A high steep bank with a broad, flat, or rounded front.
Canyon	A deep, narrow valley with precipitous sides, often with a stream flowing through it.
Fen	An alkaline wetland that is fed by ground water and is often seen as a wet meadow and characterized by plants like Grass or Parnasis and sedges that grow in alkaline water.
Forest	A vegetative community dominated by trees and many containing understory layers of smaller trees, shorter shrubs and an herbaceous layers at the ground.
Grove	A small wooded area without underbrush, such as a picnic area.
Herb	A seed producing annual, biennial, or perennial that does not develop persistent woody tissue but dies down at the end of a growing season.
Karst	An irregular limestone region with sinks, underground streams, and caverns.
Lake	A considerable inland body of standing water.
Marsh	A wetland fed by streams and with shallow or deep water. Often characterized by mats of cattail, bulrushes, sedges and wetland forbs.
Mesic	A type of plant that requires a moderate amount of water.
Moraine	Long, irregular hills of glacial till deposited by stagnant and retreating glaciers.

Explanation of Geographical Terms (continued)

Natural Community	A group of living organisms that live in the same place, e.g. woodland or prairie.
Park	An area maintained in its natural state as a public property.
Pond	A body of water usually smaller than a lake.
Prairie	Primarily treeless grassland community characterized by full sun and dominated by perennial, native grasses and forbs. Isolated remnants of tall grass prairie can be found along and near the I&M Corridor.
Preserve	An area restricted for the protection and preservation of natural resources.
Ridge	A range of hills or mountains.
Savanna	A grassland ecosystem with scattered trees characterized by native grasses and forbs.
Sedges	Grass-like plants with triangular stems and without showy flowers. Many are dominant in sedge meadows, bogs and fens but others are found in woodlands or prairies.
Shrubs	Low woody plants, usually shorter than trees and with several stems.
Swale	A lower lying or depressed and off wet stretch of land.
Swamp	Spongy land saturated and sometimes partially or intermittently covered with water.

Turf   The upper stratum of soil bound by grass and plant roots into a
            thick mat.

Wetland   The low lying wet area between higher ridges.

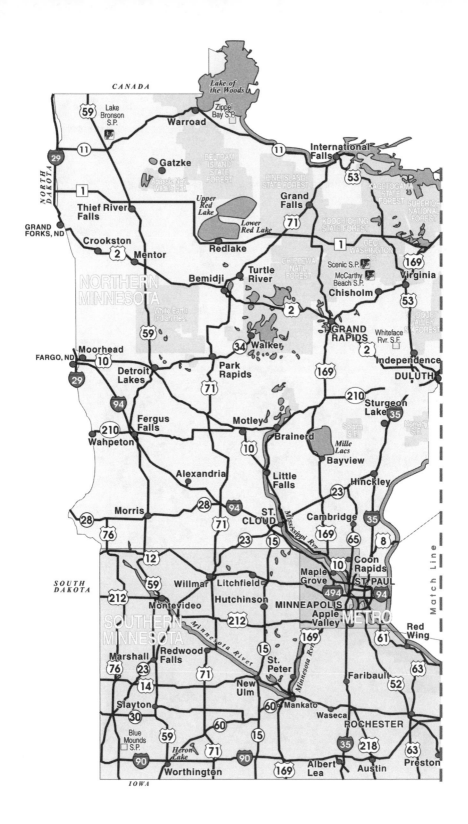

CANADA

Lake of
the Woods

NORTH DAKOTA

Lake
Bronson
S.P.

Zippel
Bay S.P.

Warroad

International
Falls

Gatzke

PINE ISLAND
STATE FOREST

BELTRAMI
ISLAND
STATE FOREST

KAGETOGAMA
STATE
FOREST

SUPERIOR
NATIONAL
FOREST

Agassiz Natl.
Wildlife Ref.

Thief River
Falls

GRAND
FORKS, ND

Upper
Red
Lake

Grand
Falls

KOOCHICHING
STATE FOREST

GEO.
WASHINGTON

Crookston

Lower
Red Lake

Mentor

Redlake

NORTHERN
MINNESOTA

Turtle
River

Bemidji

CHIPPEWA
NAT'L.
FOREST

Scenic S.P.

McCarthy
Beach S.P.

Virginia

Chisholm

White Earth
Indian Res.

Walker

GRAND
RAPIDS

Whiteface
Rvr. S.F.

LOUQUET
VALLEY
STATE
FOREST

Moorhead

FARGO, ND

Detroit
Lakes

Park
Rapids

Independence

DULUTH

Fergus
Falls

Motley

Savanna
S.P.

Sturgeon
Lake

Nemadji
S.F.

Wahpeton

Brainerd

Mille
Lacs

Alexandria

Little
Falls

Bayview

Hinckley

Morris

ST.
CLOUD

Cambridge

SOUTH
DAKOTA

Willmar

Litchfield

Maple
Grove

Coon
Rapids

ST. PAUL

Montevideo

Hutchinson

MINNEAPOLIS

METRO

SOUTHERN
MINNESOTA

Apple
Valley

Red
Wing

Marshall

Redwood
Falls

St.
Peter

Faribault

New
Ulm

Slayton

Mankato

Waseca

ROCHESTER

Blue
Mounds
S.P.

Heron
Lake

Worthington

Albert
Lea

Austin

Preston

IOWA

Match Line

Mississippi River

Minnesota River

Minnesota Rvr.

State of Minnesota

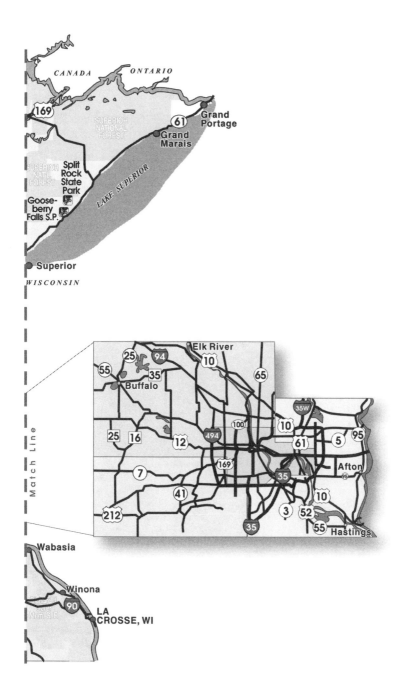

CANADA · ONTARIO

169

SUPERIOR
NATIONAL
FOREST

61 Grand
Portage

Grand
Marais

SUPERIOR
NATL
FOREST

Split
Rock
State
Park

Goose-
berry
Falls S.P.

LAKE SUPERIOR

Superior

WISCONSIN

Match Line

Elk River

25 94

55 35
Buffalo

10

65

35W

100

10

25 16

12

494

61

5 95

7

169

35

Afton

41

212

3 52

35

55 Hastings

Wabasia

Winona

90

LA
CROSSE, WI

Southern Minnesota

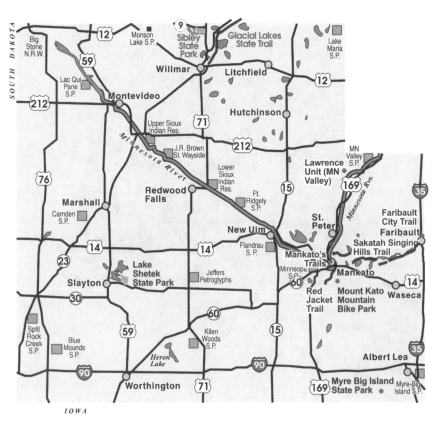

Southern Minnesota Attractions

Big Stone Wildlife Refuge 25 NW 2nd St, Ortonville
May-Sept; sunrise-sunset. Auto tours & foot trails through
refuge. Free, located SE from Hwys 75 & 12, 2+ mi.

Alexander Ramsey Park Hwy 19, Redwood Falls
Open year round, until 10pm daily. Largest municipal park
in MN with hiking & ski trails, playgrounds, campsites & an
exercise course.

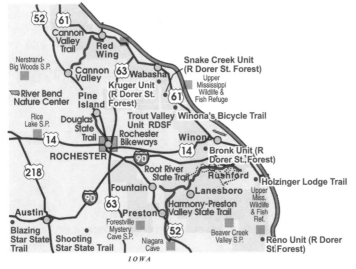

Blazing Star State Trail

Trail Length	6 miles, total of 20 miles planned
Surface	Paved, undeveloped
Uses	Leisure bicycling, cross-country skiing, in-line skating, hiking
Location & Setting	The trail runs from Albert Lea Lake in Albert Lea to Big Island State Park. It currently connects to Albert Lea's city trail system. When completed, it will connect Albert Lea and Austin via Big Island State Park and Hayward. It will eventually connect to the Shooting Star State Trail. The local setting is rural landscapes. Big Island State Park provides an opportunity to experience wetlands, oak savanna, big woods and prairie.
Information	DNR Information Center 651-296-6157 Albert Lea Parks & Recreation 507-377-4370
County	Freeborn

Parking
Albert Lea at Frank Hall Park at the trailhead
Big Island State Park at the New York Point Group Center and at the Little Island Pioneer Campground.

Sharing the Trail

- Stay on designated trail
- Keep right so others can pass
- Obey traffic signs and rules
- Pack out all garbage and litter
- Respect adjoining landowners rights and privacy
- Warn other trail users when passing by giving an audible signal
- Overnight camping and campfires are permitted only on designated campsites.
- Don't disturb the wild plants and animals.

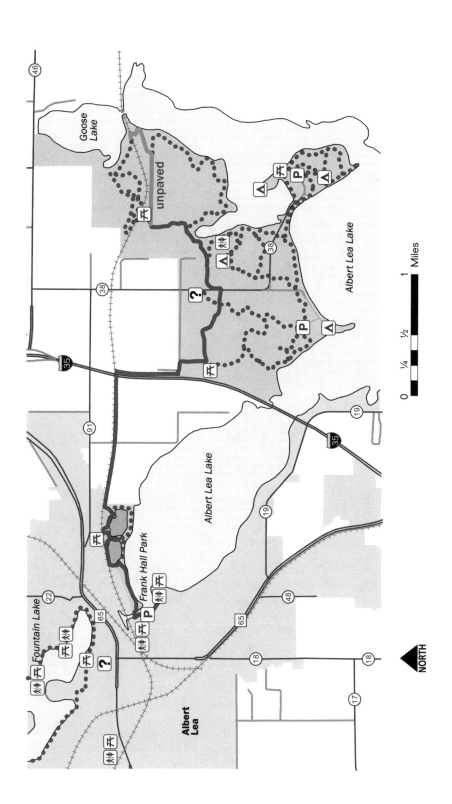

Goose Lake

unpaved

Albert Lea Lake

Albert Lea Lake

Fountain Lake

Frank Hall Park

Albert Lea

NORTH

0   ¼   ½   1   Miles

Cannon Valley Trail

Trail Length	19.7 miles
Surface	Asphalt
Uses	Leisure bicycling, cross country skiing, in-line skating, hiking
Location & Setting	The Cannon Valley Trail runs from Cannon Falls to Red Wing on an abandoned railroad line in southeastern Minnesota. There are overhanging cliffs near Cannon Falls, and the scenery is diverse and spectacular. The setting includes woods, river views, bluffs and small communities.
Information	Cannon Valley Trail Office 507-263-0508 Red Wing Chamber of Commerce 651-388-4719
County	Goodhue

WELCH The trail passes a downhill ski resort. Welch is a small village 1/3 mile north of the Welch station access (look for signs on trail). Bicycle and canoe/tube rental is available. Camping nearby at Hidden Valley Campground.

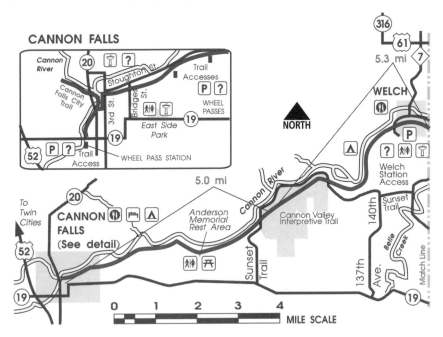

CANNON FALLS Western Trailhead is located at the ballpark on E. Stoughton St., but a trail extension continues on as the Cannon Falls City Trail for approximately 2 miles near Hwys. 19 & 20. There is parking at the trailhead, and ample facilities and shopping can be found within Cannon Falls.

Wheel passes are required if bicycling or in-line skating and age 18 or older. Available at trailside self purchase stations.

Goodhue County Historical Society 1166 Oak St, Red Wing, MN 55066 Archaeological & geological exhibits; pottery collection, Dakota tribal history, fashions, medicine & immigration period.

ROUTE SLIP	INCREMENT	TOTAL
Red Wing		
Hwy. 61	4.7	4.7
Belle Creek	3.6	8.3
Welch Station	1.4	9.7
Sunset Trail	5.0	14.7
Anderson Rest Area	1.2	15.9
Cannon Falls	3.8	19.7

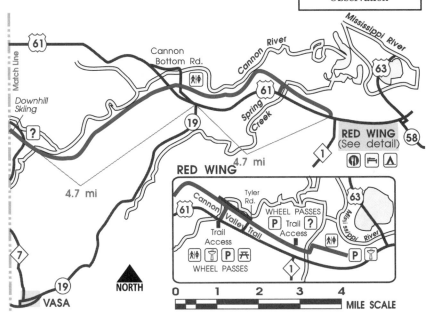

RED WING Eastern Trailhead is located on old W. Main St. at the intersection of Bench St. Red Wing is a popular tourist attraction with many antique, pottery, leather goods, woolens and doll shops. There is ample restaurants and lodgings. Bike rental is available.

Douglas State Trail

Trail Length	12.5 miles
Surface	Asphalt (with a separate turf threadway)
Uses	Leisure bicycling, cross country skiing, in-line skating, horseback riding, snowmobiling, jogging
Location & Setting	The Douglas State Trails is multi-use and was developed on abandoned railroad bed. The trail travels from northwest Rochester, through the town of Douglas, and ends at Pine Island.
Information	Douglas State Trail 507-285-7176
County	Olmsted

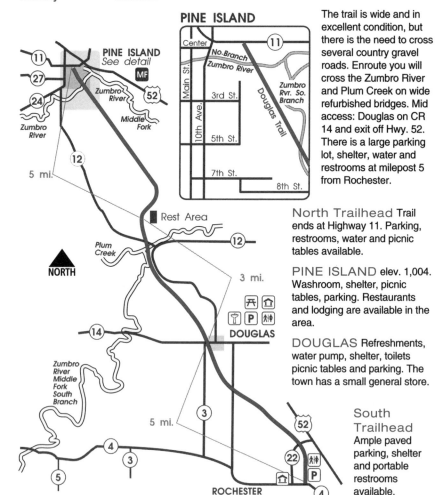

The trail is wide and in excellent condition, but there is the need to cross several country gravel roads. Enroute you will cross the Zumbro River and Plum Creek on wide refurbished bridges. Mid access: Douglas on CR 14 and exit off Hwy. 52. There is a large parking lot, shelter, water and restrooms at milepost 5 from Rochester.

North Trailhead Trail ends at Highway 11. Parking, restrooms, water and picnic tables available.

PINE ISLAND elev. 1,004. Washroom, shelter, picnic tables, parking. Restaurants and lodging are available in the area.

DOUGLAS Refreshments, water pump, shelter, toilets picnic tables and parking. The town has a small general store.

South Trailhead Ample paved parking, shelter and portable restrooms available.

22

Faribault City Trails

Trail Length	4.0 miles
Surface	Paved
Uses	Leisure bicycling, in-line skating, hiking
Location & Setting	This 4 mile paved trail follows the Straight River in Faribault from the south end of the city to the north end at 2nd Ave. NW, near Father Slevin Park. Faribault is located at the east end of Sakatah Singing Hills State Trail in south central Minnesota.
Information	Faribault Parks & Recreation 507-332-6112
County	Rice

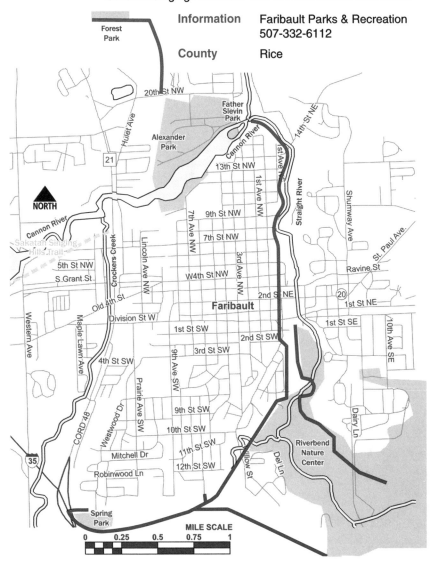

Glacial Lakes State Trail

Trail Length	36.0 miles (includes 18 miles planned)
Surface	Asphalt: 12 miles between Willmar and NE of New London. Crushed granite for 2 miles further to Hawick. Undeveloped for 22 miles between Hawick & Richmond.
Uses	Leisure bicycling, cross country skiing, in-line skating, snowmobiling, horseback riding, hiking
Location & Setting	The Glacial Lakes State Trail is built on abandoned railroad bed and is located in southwestern Minnesota between Willmar and Richmond. The topography is rolling and it cuts across the border between western tall grass prairie and eastern deciduous forest. Farmland, virgin prairie remnants and scattered wood lots.
Information	New London Trail Office 320-354-4940
Counties	Kandiyohi, Stearns

Parking Facilities

Willmar - take Highway 12 east to County Road 9. Turn left (north) and go 2 miles to the Civic Center.

SPICER junction of Highway 23 and County Road 10. Parking is off 23.

NEW LONDON From Highway 23, follow Highway 9 north to parking and public water access on the east.

REGAL

Sibley State Park

Mud Lake

NEW LONDON

Norway Lake

Andrew Lake

U = Unpaved
A = Asphalt

SPICER

WILLMAR

KANDIYOHI

NORTH

MILE SCALE
0 1 2 3 4

Match Line

See Inset

24

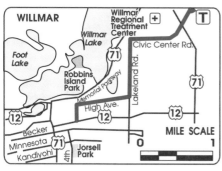

No snowmobile use is allowed on the undeveloped trail in Steam's County.

ROSCOE

COLD SPRING MF

23

RICHMOND

Stearns County
Kandiyohi County

66

Rice Lake

PAYNESVILLE
MF

22

HAWICK

Lake Koronis

Stearns County
Meeker County

66

Lake Koronis Regional Park

EDEN VALLEY

NORTH

22

The Glacial Lakes State Trail connects to Sibley State Park via 3 miles of paved shoulder along Route 9. The trail also connects with many miles of groomed snowmobile trails.

Kandiyohi County
Meeker County

ATWATER

GROVE CITY

Match Line

TRAILS MILEAGE CHART	Spicer	New London	Hawick	Sibley SP	Paynesville	Richmond
Willmar	6.5	12.0	18.0	16.0	22.5	36.0
Spicer		5.5	11.5	9.5	16.0	30.5
New London			6.0	4.0	10.5	24.0
Hawick				10.0	4.5	18.0
Sibley State Park					14.5	28.0
Paynesville						13.5

Lake Shetek State Park

Trail Length	6.0 miles
Surface	Paved
Uses	Leisure bicycling, in-line skating, cross-county skiing, hiking
Location & Setting	The paved trail runs from Currie north for 3 miles to the park and continues for another 3-miles within the park. Lake Shetek SP facilities include a swimming beach, boating, canoeing, and fishing. There are 108 campsites.
Information	Lake Shetek State Park 507-763-3256
Counties	Murray

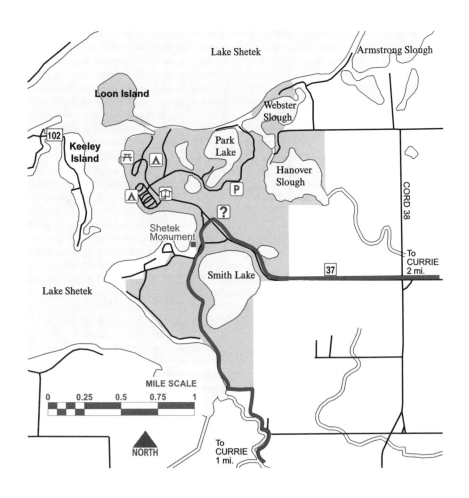

Mankato City Trails

Trail Length	7.0 miles
Surface	Paved
Uses	Leisure bicycling, in-line skating, cross-country skiing, hiking
Location & Setting	Several unconnected segments make up these 7 miles of city off-road trail. One segment connects to the Red Jacket Trail. There is a sidewalk/street connection to the Sakatah Singing Hills Trail from the trail segment along Belgrade Ave.
Information	Mankato Parks Dept. 507-387-8649
Counties	Blue Earth

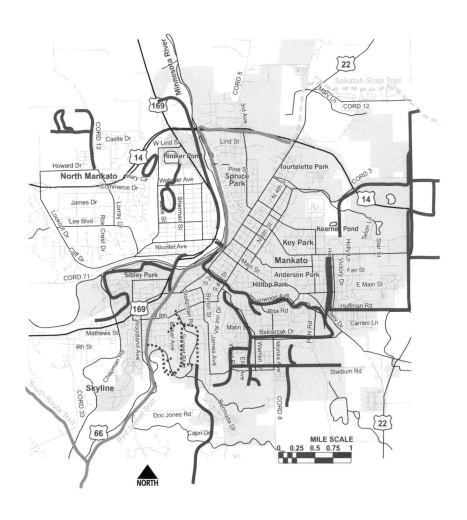

Red Jacket Trail

Trail Length	6.0 miles
Surface	Paved
Uses	Leisure bicycling, cross country skiing, in-line skating, jogging
Location & Setting	The Red Jacket Trail is built on abandoned railroad from the River Front Drive in Mankato to Rapidan. It passes the Mt. Kato ski area and mountain bike park and over three railroad trestles and through farmland to County Route 9 in the village of Rapidan. From there you can take a paved shoulder for another two mile west on CR 9 to Rapidan Dam park. Setting is urban, countryside and wooded hillside.
Information	Blue Earth County Highway & Park Department 507- 625-3281
County	Blue Earth

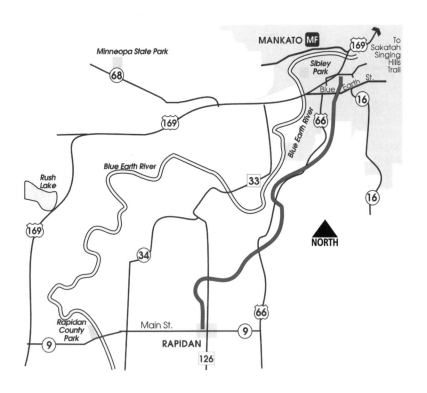

Minnesota offers varied terrains for biking because it is situated at an ecological crossroads for three regions - the western plains and prairies, the northern coniferous forest and the eastern hardwood forest.

The plains area covers the northwestern strip of Minnesota along its Red River Valley border and most of the southwestern quarter of the state. Here, cyclists can expect to find mostly level terrain, with only occasional hilly areas. It is largely farmland, with isolated wooded areas and tree-lined rivers.

The north central and northeastern areas of Minnesota are very wooded, with pine or pine/hardwood mixed forests, dotted with thousands of sparkling lakes. The region is noted for its many resorts and recreational opportunities. The terrain is gently rolling. The very northeast 'Arrowhead' tip of the state has some steeper hills that line the North Shore of Lake Superior.

The southeastern quarter of the state was once covered by a great hardwood forest, most of it cleared years ago for farming. The area is now gently rolling farmland, with many lakes and rivers and stands of hardwood forest. The extreme southeastern corner of the state is an area of rounded bluffs, valleys bordering meandering streams, and sheer limestone cliffs. Its hills offer some of the most challenging biking in Minnesota, and also some of the most beautiful.

Information

Minnesota State Bicycle Coordinator	651-297-2136
Minnesota Dept. of Natural Resources	888-646-6367
Minnesota Dept. of Transportation	800-657-3774
Minnesota Dept. of Public Safety	651-201-7000

River Bend Nature Center

Trail Length	10.0 miles
Surface	Packed dirt
Uses	Leisure bicycling, cross country skiing, hiking
Location & Setting	The River Bend Nature Center is located in Faribault about 50 miles south of Minneapolis/St. Paul. The setting includes forest, prairie, wetland and riverbank.
Information	River Bend Nature Center 507-332-7151
County	Rice

River Bend Nature Center

East of Faribault Regional Center on Rustad Rd. 661 acres with some 8 miles of trails. Restrooms and picnic areas

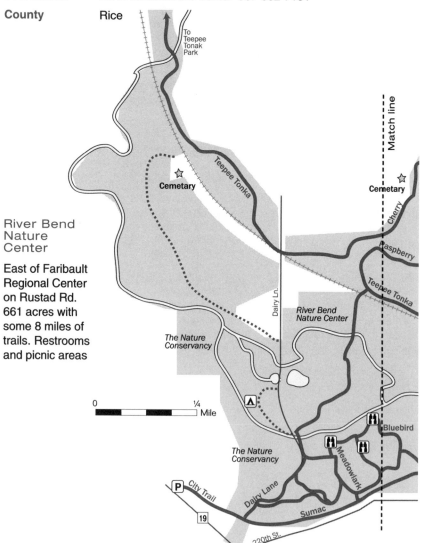

All trails are open to bicycles except a small area of handicapped accessible trails around the Trailside Center, a nature study center.

Eastern Trailhead at 7th Avenue. Parking available about one mile west near a Dairy Queen on north side of HWY 60 near I-35 exit. Multiple services nearby.

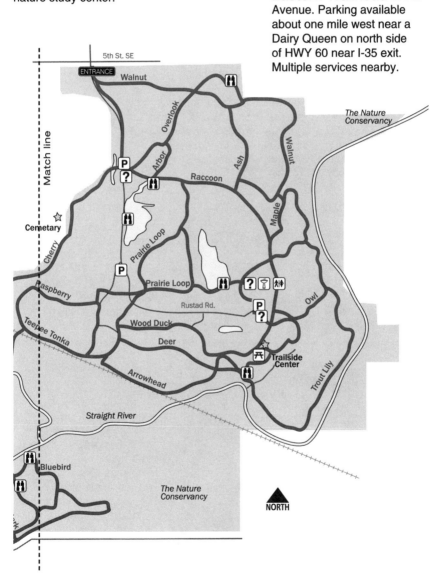

Southern Minnesota Science & Nature Centers

Quarry Hill Nature Center 701 Silver Creek Rd NE, Rochester
Open year round, M-Sat 8-4:30; Sun 12-4:30. Caves, quarry, stream & trails.
Free admission & parking. Located near 4th St S & Co Rd 22 (E Circle Dr).

Museum of Natural History Dept of Biology, SW State Univ., Marshall
Open M-F 8-4:30 during academic year. Flora and fauna exhibits of southwestern
MN. Free admission & parking. Located N of Hwy 19 on Hwy 23.

Dale A Gardner Aerospace Museum & Learning Center
112 N Main, Sherburn
Summer, M-F 1-5, Sat 9-5, or by appointment. Suit worn by Gardner on shuttle,
heat shield tiles, stardome, library & space videos. Free admission & parking. Take
exit 87 at I-90 & 4.

J.C. Hormel Nature Center Box 673, Austin
M-Sat 9-5 (closed 12-1) Sun 1-5. Woods, prairie. .5 mi of asphalt trail allows wheel-
chairs, strollers, etc. into preserve. 278 acres with 7.5 mi of walking trails. Free
admission & parking. 1/4 mi N of I-90E on exit 218.

Southern Minnesota Attractions

Big Stone County Historical Museum
RR 2, Box 31, Ortonville
Year round, T-F 11-4 May-Sept: S&S 1-4. Historic boat, Native American photographer Roland Reed photos, caskets; historic flags & more. Admission fee, Free parking. Junction of US 12 & 75.

Freeborn County Historical Museum & Pioneer Village
1031 Bridge Ave N, Albert Lea
Museum, library, 1880s village, log cabins, school, church, blacksmith, PO & shops. Open year round. Admission Free, Free parking. 2 mi S of I-90, near fairgrounds, Exit #157.

Rochester Trails & Bikeways

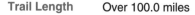

Trail Length	Over 100.0 miles
Surface	Asphalt paths and designated streets
Uses	Leisure bicycling, in-line skating, jogging
Location & Setting	Rochester is located in southeastern Minnesota. It has an excellent system of bicycle trails along the waterways and through it's many parks.
Information	Rochester Parks & Recreations 507-281-6160
Counties	Olmsted

Rochester Area Attractions

Heritage House of Rochester 225 First Av NW Rochester, MN 55903
Located in Central Park, an 1856 town square. Exhibits life of midwestern family 150 years ago, restored house authentically furnished with antiques, quilts, dolls, garden, etc.

Olmsted County History Center 1195 Co Rd 22 SW, Rochester, MN 55902
History of Rochester and surrounding area; research library/archives with over 600,000 maps, photographs, diaries, etc. relating primarily to Olmsted County and southeastern MN.

 BIKE ROUTE SIGNS identify on-road routes usually connecting or leading to off-road facilities.

 BIKE PATH SIGNS identify off-road facilities.

 BIKE LANE SIGNS identify a designated lane for bicycles usually on the right side of the roadway.

Bicycle licenses are required and are available at local license bureaus and at several bike shops.

Bicycle signs identify off-road trails, on-road routes and designated bike lanes.

Bicycle parking racks are provided in most municipal lots and at various locations in the downtown area.

Map on following page

Rochester Trails & Bikeways (continued)

Mayo Clinic

The largest medical complex in the world, the Mayo Clinic is reflected in it's diagnostic resources, educational and research facilities.

There is a twenty minute informational film shown weekdays at 10:00 a.m. and again at 2:00 p.m. in the Judd Hall subway level of the Mayo Building.

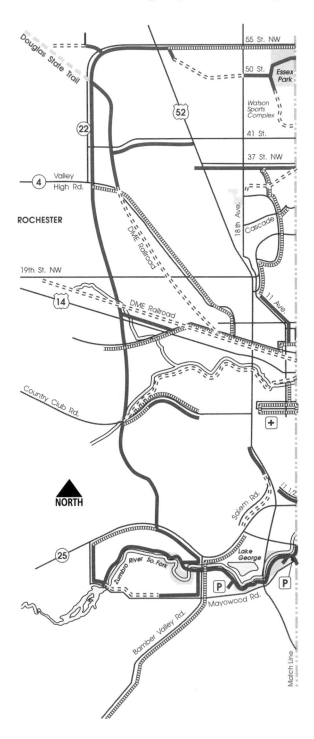

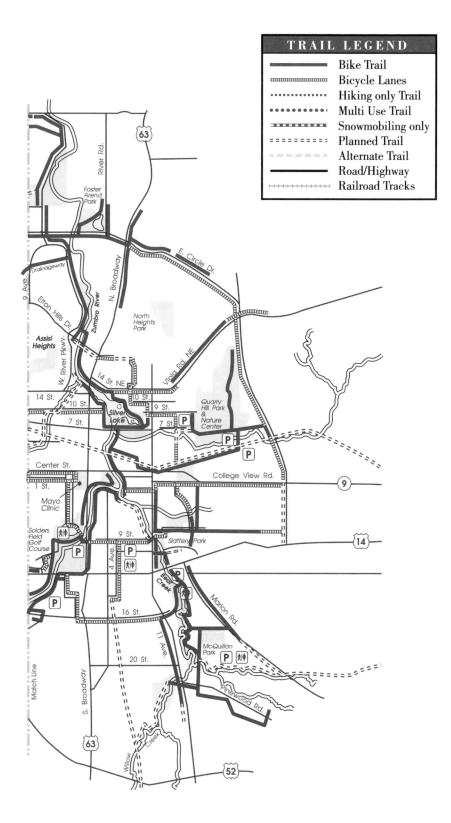

TRAIL LEGEND

————	Bike Trail
▭▭▭▭▭	Bicycle Lanes
············	Hiking only Trail
••••••••••	Multi Use Trail
▬ ▬ ▬ ▬ ▬	Snowmobiling only
= = = = = =	Planned Trail
▭ ▭ ▭ ▭ ▭	Alternate Trail
————	Road/Highway
┼┼┼┼┼┼┼┼┼┼	Railroad Tracks

River Rd.

63

Foster Arend Park

E. Circle Dr.

9 Ave.

Drainageway

Elton Hills Dr.

N. Broadway

Zumbro River

North Heights Park

Assisi Heights

W. River Pkwy.

14 St. NE

Viola Rd. NE

14 St.   10 St.   10 St.

9 St.   Quarry Hill Park & Nature Center

Silver Lake   7 St.   7 St.   P

P

P

Center St.   College View Rd.

1 St.   9

Mayo Clinic

Solders Field Golf Course   9 St.   Slattery Park

P   P   14

4 Ave.   P   Bear Creek

P   Marion Rd.

16 St.

11 Ave.

McQuillan Park   P

20 St.

Pinewood Rd.

Match Line

S. Broadway

63

Willow Creek

52

35

Root River Trail

Trail Length	42.0 miles
Surface	Asphalt
Uses	Leisure bicycling, cross country skiing, in-line skating, hiking
Location & Setting	Located in southeastern Minnesota between Fountain and Houston, the Root River Trail provides outstanding views of the soaring limestone bluffs of the Root River Valley. It was developed on abandoned railroad grade. Wildlife is abundant and sightings of wild turkey, deer, hawks and turkey vultures are common. Historical buildings and rural communities along the trail provide sites of interest to trail users. Services to be found include campgrounds, bed and breakfast inns, restaurants, museums, outfitters and unique stores.
Information	Lanesboro Trail Office 507-467-2552
Counties	Fillmore, Houston

Harmony–Preston Valley State Trail

Trail Length	18.0 miles
Surface	Asphalt
Uses	Leisure bicycling, cross country skiing, in-line skating, hiking
Location & Setting	The trail connects the communities of Harmony and Preston with the Root River Trail. The northern two-thirds of the Harmony-Preston Valley State Trail follows and crosses Watson Creek, the South Branch of the Root River, and Camp Creek, passing through a variety of wooded areas and farmland on an abandoned railroad grade. The southern third of the trail between Preston and Harmony climbs out of the valley and travels along a ridge line between valleys.
Information	Historic Bluff Country 800-428-2030
County	Fillmore

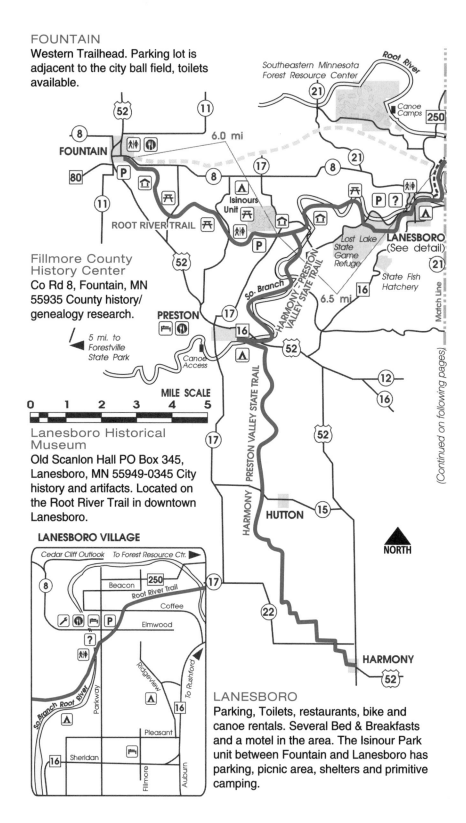

FOUNTAIN
Western Trailhead. Parking lot is adjacent to the city ball field, toilets available.

Southeastern Minnesota Forest Resource Center

Canoe Camps

6.0 mi

FOUNTAIN

ROOT RIVER TRAIL

Isinours Unit

Lost Lake State Game Refuge

LANESBORO (See detail)

State Fish Hatchery

6.5 mi

Fillmore County History Center
Co Rd 8, Fountain, MN 55935 County history/ genealogy research.

PRESTON

5 mi. to Forestville State Park

So. Branch

HARMONY - PRESTON VALLEY STATE TRAIL

Canoe Access

MILE SCALE
0 1 2 3 4 5

Lanesboro Historical Museum
Old Scanlon Hall PO Box 345, Lanesboro, MN 55949-0345 City history and artifacts. Located on the Root River Trail in downtown Lanesboro.

HUTTON

NORTH

HARMONY

(Continued on following pages)

Match Line

LANESBORO VILLAGE

Cedar Cliff Outlook   To Forest Resource Ctr.

Beacon

Root River Trail

Coffee

Elmwood

Ridgeview

To Rushford

Parkway

So. Branch Root River

Pleasant

Sheridan

Fillmore

Auburn

LANESBORO
Parking, Toilets, restaurants, bike and canoe rentals. Several Bed & Breakfasts and a motel in the area. The Isinour Park unit between Fountain and Lanesboro has parking, picnic area, shelters and primitive camping.

Root River Trail & Harmony-Preston Valley State Trail (continued)

ROUTE SLIP	INCREMENT	TOTAL	ELEV.
Money Creek	5.8	5.8	
Rushford	4.8	10.6	726
Peterson	8.9	19.5	761
Whalen	4.6	25.1	792
Lanesboro	4.7	29.8	846
Isinours Unit	5.5	35.3	
Fountain	6.5	41.8	1,305

1877 Peterson Station Museum
228 Mill St, Peterson, MN 55962 Local memorabelia, artifacts, photos, original depot built in 1877; was part of the former Southern MN RR.

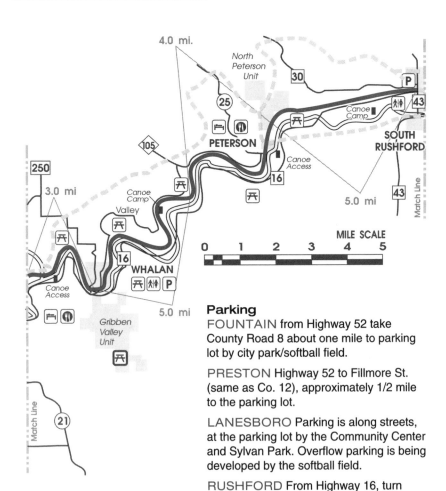

Parking

FOUNTAIN from Highway 52 take County Road 8 about one mile to parking lot by city park/softball field.

PRESTON Highway 52 to Fillmore St. (same as Co. 12), approximately 1/2 mile to the parking lot.

LANESBORO Parking is along streets, at the parking lot by the Community Center and Sylvan Park. Overflow parking is being developed by the softball field.

RUSHFORD From Highway 16, turn north on Elm Street, go one block Parking lot is by depot.

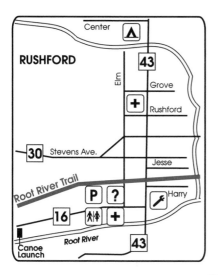

RUSHFORD Parking, toilets, restaurants, picnic area and canoe rentals near the old train depot at the trailhead. There are 46 bridges along the Root River Trail, with one approximately 500 feet long. In addition to biking, there is ample opportunities for canoeing or fishing.

There is no fee for state trail use.

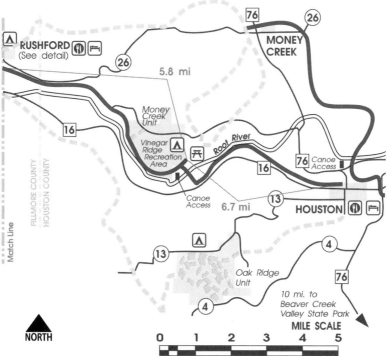

Nearby Area Attractions

Harmony Toy Museum 30 S Main, Harmony, MN 55939
Antiques & new items, many handmade, cast iron toy farm machinery, trains.

Historic Forestville Rt 2 Box 126, Preston, MN 55965
Village restored to 1899; store/post office, Thomas J. Meighen's residence; costumed guides depicting daily lives.

Sakatah Singing Hills State Trail

Trail Length	39.0 miles
Surface	Asphalt
Uses	Leisure bicycling, cross country skiing, in-line skating
Location & Setting	The Sakatah Singing Hills Trail is located between Mankato and Faribault in south central Minnesota It was developed on abandoned railroad grade. This level trail wanders along pastures, farmland, several lakes, and a forested park.
Information	Sakatah Singing Hills Trail 507-267-4774 Mankato Chamber of Commerce 507-345-4519
Counties	Rice, LeSueur, Blue Earth

Sakatah Singing Hills State Trail Area Attractions

Alexander Faribault House 121st Ave NE, Faribault, MN 55021-5226
Historic 1853 residence, period furnishings, some original belongings; Alexander Faribault helped establish Minnesota as a state.

Blue Earth County Historical Society 416 Cherry St., Mankato, MN 56001
Located at the Heritage Center; museum hightlights settlement, history and culture of Blue Earth County and Mankato, with artifacts from Blue Earth County Historical Society Collection.

MN Valley Regional Library-Maud Hart Lovelace Collection
100 Main St E., Mankato, MN 56001
Children's books items of interest including large mural, original drawings, autographed collection, slide-tape presentation and many items of memorabilia.

Le Sueur Cty History Society Museum 2nd & Frank St., Elysian, MN 56028
County history; famous area artists; genealogy center; post office, county schoolroom, military exhibit, church room.

Le Sueur City Museum 709 2nd St N., Le Sueur, MN 56058
Located in the old Union School building, built in 1872, burned down and rebuilt in 1911. Features include nearly 100 years of Green Giant Company history; veterinary office with pharmacy, old hotel, musical instruments, paintings by local artists, high school class photos, family research center, agricultural & military exhibits.

R. D. Hubbard House 606 Broad St S., Mankato, MN 56001
Victorian 1871 Second Empire mansion, carriage house, formal gardens.

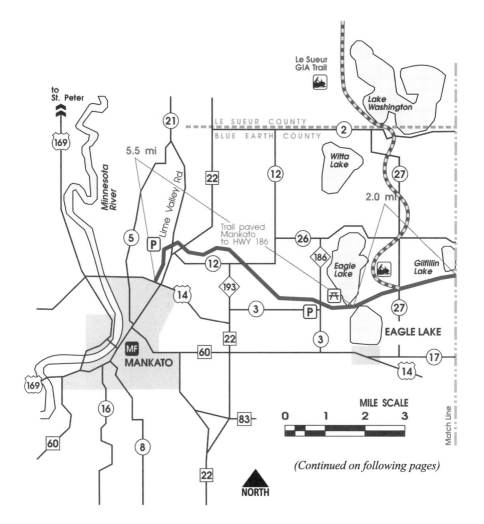

to St. Peter

Le Sueur
GIA Trail

Lake Washington

LE SUEUR COUNTY
BLUE EARTH COUNTY

Minnesota River

5.5 mi

Lime Valley Rd

Witta Lake

Trail paved
Mankato
to HWY 186

2.0 mi

Eagle Lake

Gilfillin Lake

EAGLE LAKE

MF
MANKATO

MILE SCALE

0   1   2   3

Match Line

(Continued on following pages)

NORTH

Western Trailhead is in Mankato. The trail proceeds south under HWY 14 for some three blocks before it ends near the intersection of HWY 14 and HWY 22. There are ample facilities throughout Mankato.

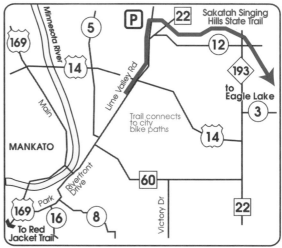

Sakatah Singing Hills State Trail

Minnesota River

to Eagle Lake

Lime Valley Rd

Trail connects to city bike paths

Main

MANKATO

Riverfront Drive

Victory Dr

Park

To Red Jacket Trail

41

The trail parallels HWY 60 just north of the road as you proceed west from Elysian. Food and lodging available in town. Parking, picnic area, and shelter available in park.

MADISON LAKE has a historic station house. There is parking, food, and gift stores nearby.

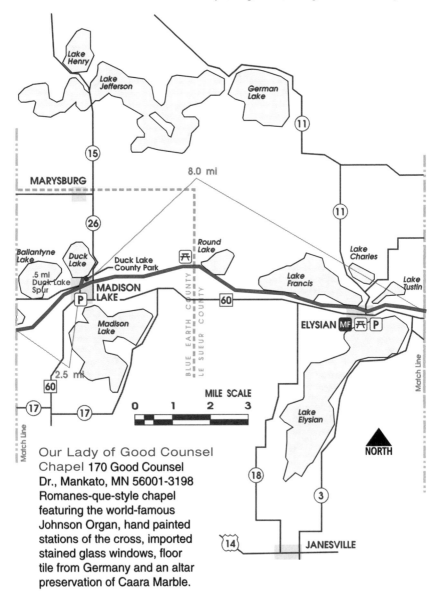

Our Lady of Good Counsel Chapel 170 Good Counsel Dr., Mankato, MN 56001-3198 Romanes-que-style chapel featuring the world-famous Johnson Organ, hand painted stations of the cross, imported stained glass windows, floor tile from Germany and an altar preservation of Caara Marble.

A one mile secondary bike path provides access into Morristown. As you enter town, observe the historic old mill and dam. Restaurant and groceries available.

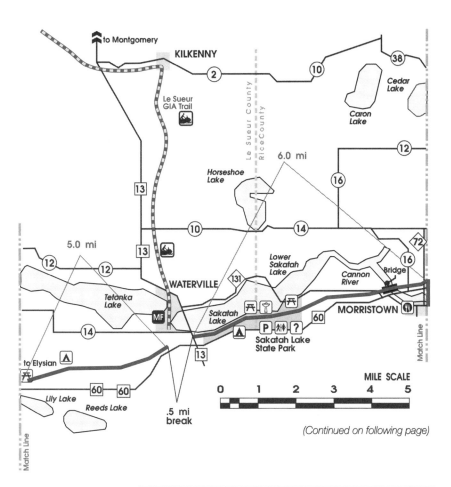

(Continued on following page)

The trail ends east of Waterville and picks up again west at Pick Street just a little north of Common St. Enter Waterville by car by exiting HWY 60 north onto HWY 13. Parking, restaurants, restrooms, and lodging available.

ROUTE SLIP	INCREMENT	TOTAL	ELEV.
Faribault			999
Warsaw	6.5	5.5	
HWY 72	2.5	9.0	1000
(to Morristown)	(1.0)		
Trail Break	.5		
Waterville	6.0	15.0	1010
Elysian (HWY 11)	5.5	20.5	
Madison Lake (HWY26)	7.5	28.0	1050
Eagle Lake	4.5	32.5	
Mankato	5.5	38.0	794

FARIBAULT

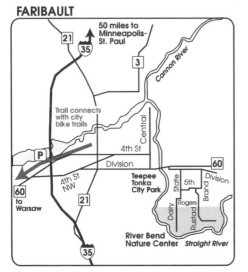

Rice County Historical Society Museum
1814 2nd Ave NW, Faribault, MN 55021
Rice County history from early American Indian times to Rice County pioneers, turn-of-the-century Main St, slide show; nearby log cabin, one-room schoolhouse, historic frame church, two agricultural and industrial buildings, genealogical research.

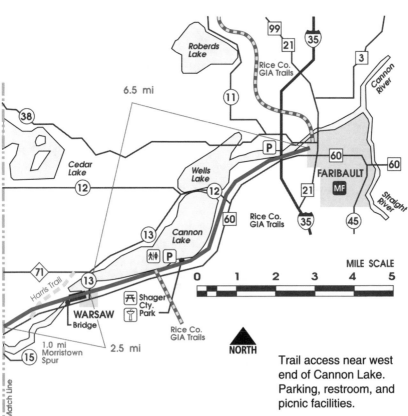

Trail access near west end of Cannon Lake. Parking, restroom, and picnic facilities.

Shooting Star State Trail

Trail Length	8 miles
Surface	Paved
Uses	Leisure bicycling, cross-country skiing, in-line skating, hiking
Location & Setting	The trail begins in the city of LeRoy in Mower County and travels north through Lake Louise State Park, then heads west towards Taopi. The setting is rural landscape, with native wildflowers and grasses bordering much of the trail. It passes by several other interpretive/recreational areas including Rustic Retreat Wildlife Management Area, Shooting Star Prairie Scientific and Natural Area, and Mower County Natural and Scenic Area. The trail parallels Hwy 56, and when completed will connect the towns of LeRoy, Taopi, Adams, Rose Creek, Austin, Lyle, and eventually Blazing Star State Trail.
Information	DNR Information Center 651-296-6157
Counties	Mower

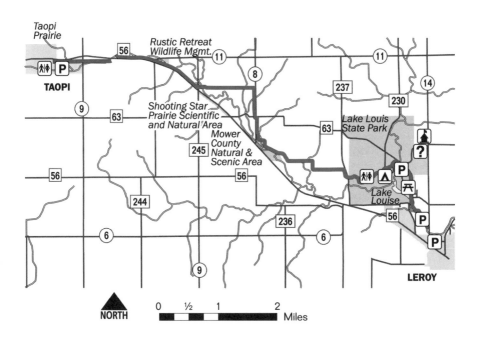

Parking
LeRoy east of CR 14 on Lowell Street.
Rowe Pit north of LeRoy off CR 14.

45

Sibley State Park

Trail Length	5.0 miles
Surface	Paved
Uses	Leisure bicycling, cross country skiing, in-line skating, hiking
Location & Setting	Sibley State Park is located in Kandiyohi County in west central Minnesota, four miles west of New London. Exit Highway 71 to road 48, which is the main entrance. The park consists of 2,300 acres, and is wooded and hilly.
Information	Sibley State Park Manager 320-354-2055
County	Kandiyohi

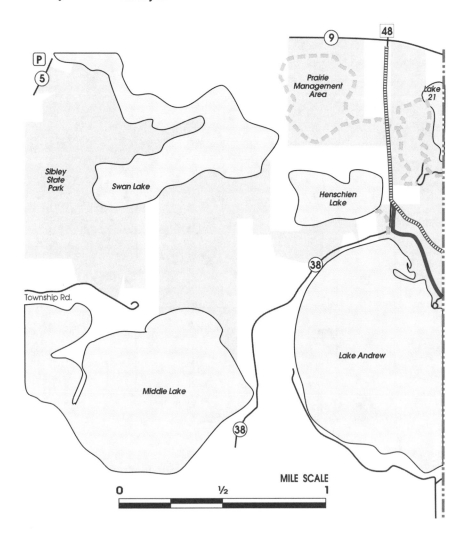

Sibley State Park was named after Henry Hastings Sibley, Minnesota's first governor. The park is located in an area where the grasslands of the west meet the big woods of the east. Mt. Tom is the highest point within 50 miles, affording an excellent view of surrounding forest, prairie knolls, lakes and farmland.

Facilities include
18 miles of hiking trail
10 miles of cross-country ski trail
9 miles of horseback riding trail and group camp
6 miles of snowmobile trail
Campsites, picnic area, swimming beach
Canoe rentals
Park store

TRAIL LEGEND

————————	Bike Trail
⊏⊏⊏⊏⊏⊏⊏⊏⊏	Bicycle Lanes
············	Hiking only Trail
●●●●●●●●●●	Multi Use Trail
▬▬▬▬▬▬	Snowmobiling only
=========	Planned Trail
▬ ▬ ▬ ▬ ▬	Alternate Trail
————————	Road/Highway
⊢⊢⊢⊢⊢⊢⊢⊢⊢	Railroad Tracks

9
71
9
Lake 21
Sibley State Park
Mt. Tom
Mt. Tom Trail
Sibley State Park
Oak Ridge
Parker-Fremberg Trail
Little Mt. Tom
Oak Hills Trail
Mt. Tom Trail
?
Pondview Trail
71
Cedar Hill
?
Lakeview Trail
48
To NEW LONDON 4 miles
Lake Andrew
To WILLMAR 15 miles
NORTH

Winona's Bicycle Trail

Trail Length	5.5 miles
Surface	Asphalt
Uses	Leisure bicycling, cross country skiing, in-line skating, jogging
Location & Setting	City of Winona in southeastern Minnesota. The trail forms two loops surrounding Lake Winona. The trail head is located at the information center on Huff Road, just east of Highway 61. Open park area, some tree shading, continuous lake views.
Information	Winona Visitors Bureau 507-452-0735
County	Winona

In addition to the bike path, some of the streets in town are designated bike routes. Winona is on the Bike Centennial route and is close to the Root River State Trail and the Great River Trail (in Wisconsin). Bike rentals are available at the bike store on Center Street.

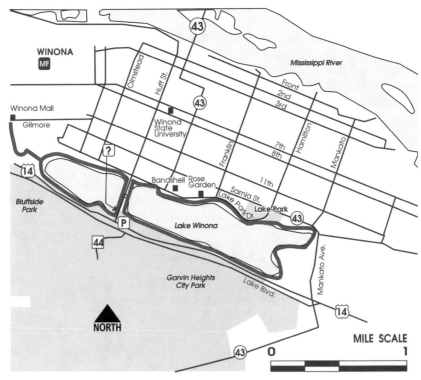

Bunnell House Museum 160 Johnson St., Winona, MN 55987
Rural gothic wood frame home built in 1850s, overlooks Mississippi River.
Winona County Historical Museum 160 Johnson St, Winona, MN 55987
American Indian exhibit, county history, Mississippi River history, archives.

Twin Cities Metro

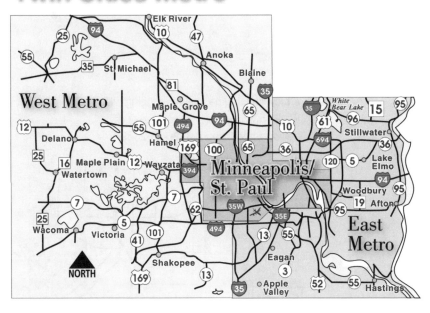

Useful Phone Number for the Minneapolis – St. Paul Area

Emergency	Police, Fire, Sheriff, Medical	911
	Road Condition Information	(800) 857-3774

General Information

City Line	Sports, weather, recreation, restaurants, buses, etc. (612) 645-6000
The Connection	Restaurants, business, entertainment, sports, live theater (612) 922-9000
Ticketmaster	Tickets for sporting events, concerts, theater, special events (612) 371-2000
Time and Weather	(612) 452-2323

Minneapolis Loop

Trail Length	38.0 miles
Surface	Asphalt
Uses	Leisure bicycling, in-line skating, jogging/hiking
Information	Minneapolis Public Works 612-673-2411
	Fort Snelling State Park 612-725-2389
Counties	Hennepin

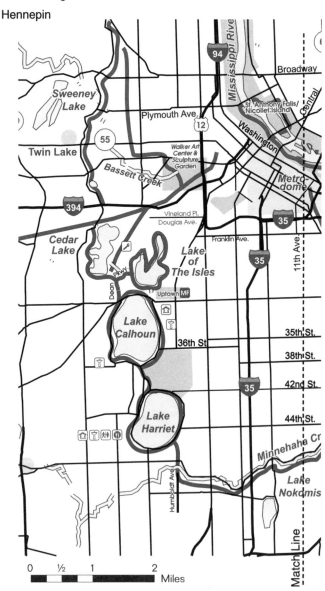

The Minneapolis Loop

Almost 40 miles long, this urban route shows off the major highlights of the city. It passes by the Walker Art Center/Guthrie Theatre, and the sculpture garden. It travels through Loring Park, along Loring Greenway, by Orchestra Hall and along Nicollet Mall, one of the largest downtown malls in the nation. After crossing the Mississippi River on the Third Ave. Bridge, the route leads to the University of Minnesota (Minneapolis Campus). The route returns to Fort Snelling State Park at the confluence of the Minnesota and Mississippi Rivers.

Wirth-Memorial Parkway

Victory Memorial Drive provides pathways for walking and biking and an opportunity for pleasure driving between Theodore Wirth Regional Park on the western edge of Minneapolis and Webber Parkway at Irving Ave. North near 45th Ave. in north Minneapolis. Hours are 6 a.m. to midnight. Facilities include biking, hiking, cross-country skiing.

Fort Snelling State Park Access

Take State Highway 5 to Post Road exit to reach the park. Post Road enters the park and serves as a bicycle route into the airport.

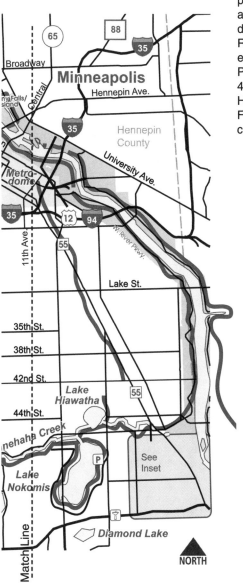

MINNEAPOLIS LOOP TRAIL HEAD

Minneapolis Parks

Minnehaha Parkway A parkway with bicycle trails and walking paths stretching from the southeast end of lake Harriet to Hiawatha Ave. Hours are from 6 a.m. to midnight. Park facilities include biking, creative play areas, hiking, cross-country skiing.

Mississippi Gorge Walking, biking trails on East and West River Parkways from Washington Ave. Bridge to Minnehaha Falls in Minneapolis. Hours on the Minneapolis side are 6 a.m. to midnight and on the St. Paul side from sunrise to sunset. Facilities include biking, hiking, cross-country skiing.

Central Mississippi Riverfront East and West side of River from Plymouth Ave. Bridge to Portland Ave. in Minneapolis. Hours are 6 a.m. to midnight. Facilities include biking, boat launching, fishing, hiking, picnic areas, power boating.

St. Paul's Area Attractions

Alexander Ramsey House 265 S Exchange St, St Paul, MN 55102 1872 home of governor, senator, & sec'y of war Alexander Ramsey; original interior, furnishings; reservations recommended.

Confederate Air Force Hangar #3 Fleming Field, South St. Paul, MN 55075. Aviation artifacts, WWII vehicles & aircraft: B-25, PBY-6A, Harvard MkIV and more.

Dakota County Historical Museum 130 3rd Ave N, South St Paul, MN 55075. Exhibits on county history; research center and cultural events.

Historic Fort Snelling Hwys 5 and 55, St Paul, MN 55111. Historic 1820s fort fully restored.

James J. Hill House 240 Summit Ave, St Paul, MN 55102. Elaborate, 32-room 1891 mansion of James J. Hill; see the art gallery, living quarters, work areas, etc.

Landmark Center #404 75 5th St W, St Paul, MN 55102. Restored Federal Courts Building, built in 1902, programs include performing and visual arts, civic activities.

Minnesota History Center 345 Kellogg Blvd W, St Paul, MN 55102. Museum, restaurant, research center in beautiful setting overlooking downtown St. Paul.

Minnesota State Capitol 75 Constitution Ave, St Paul, MN 55155. Beautiful1905 capitol by Cass Gilbert (architect of the U.S. Supreme Court Bldg) marble dome is one of largest in the world.

Old Muskego Church 2481 Como Ave, St Paul, MN 55108. Built by Norwegian immigrants in 1843, moved to current site, Luther Seminary, in 1904; inquire at Information in Campus Center.

Trains at Bandana Twin City Model Railroad Club 1021 Bandana Blvd E, Bandana Square, St Paul, MN 55108. 0-scale model railroad layout of the 1930s, 40s & 50s, with landmarks, artifacts.

Minnesota Air Guard Museum Minneapolis Air Guard Base MSP IAP, St Paul, MN 55111. Aircraft, photographs, artifacts tell the history of the Minnesota Air National Guard; A-12 Blackbird.

St. Paul Loop

Trail Length	33.0 miles
Surface	Paved
Uses	Leisure bicycling, in-line skating, jogging
Location & Setting	The "St. Paul Loop" starts in Fort Snelling State Park. Proceed northwest on Minnehaha Ave. through Minnehaha Park. Cross the Ford Bridge to the east bank of the Mississippi River to Hidden Falls Park. The route takes you to the University of Minnesota (St. Paul Campus) through the Minnesota State Fairgrounds to Como Park to Lake Phalen Park. It then follows Johnson Parkway to Indian Mounds Regional Park where you will find excellent views of the Mississippi River and large American Indian Burial Mounds. The Kellog Street Bridge leads into downtown St. Paul.
Information	St Paul Parks & Recreation 651-266-6400
Counties	Ramsey

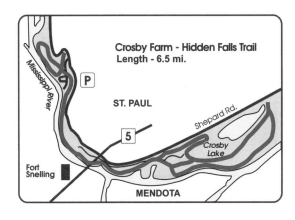

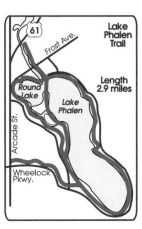

AREA LEGEND

- City, Town
- Parks, Preserves
- Waterway
- Marsh/Wetland
- Mileage Scale
- ★ Points of Interest
- – – County/State
- Forest/Woods

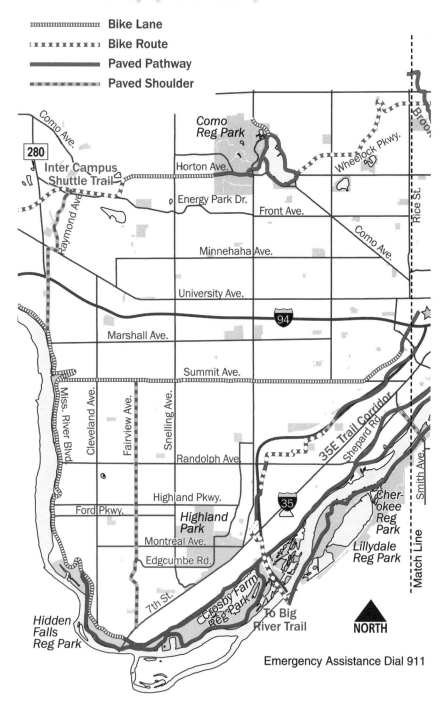

Bike Lane
Bike Route
Paved Pathway
Paved Shoulder

Como Ave.
280
Inter Campus
Shuttle Trail
Raymond Ave.

Como Reg Park
Horton Ave.
Energy Park Dr.
Front Ave.
Minnehaha Ave.
University Ave.
Marshall Ave.
Summit Ave.

Wheelock Pkwy.
Como Ave.
Rice St.
Brook

94

Miss. River Blvd.
Cleveland Ave.
Fairview Ave.
Snelling Ave.
Randolph Ave.
Highland Pkwy.
Ford Pkwy.
Highland Park
Montreal Ave.
Edgcumbe Rd.
7th St.

35E Trail Corridor
Shepard Rd.
Smith Ave.

35

Cher-
okee
Reg
Park
Lillydale
Reg Park

Match Line

Crosby Farm
Reg Park
To Big
River Trail

Hidden
Falls
Reg Park

NORTH

Emergency Assistance Dial 911

54

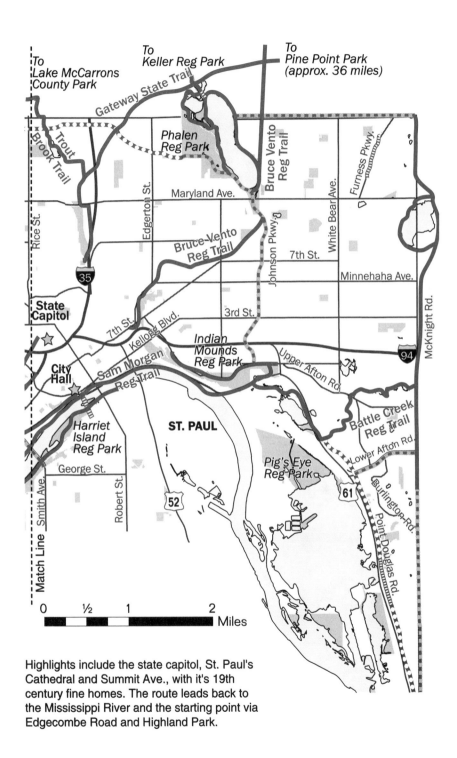

To
Lake McCarrons
County Park

To
Keller Reg Park

To
Pine Point Park
(approx. 36 miles)

Gateway State Trail

Trout Brook Trail

Phalen Reg Park

Bruce Vento Reg Trail

Furness Pkwy.

Rice St.

Edgerton St.

Maryland Ave.

Bruce Vento Reg Trail

Johnson Pkwy.

White Bear Ave.

35

7th St.

Minnehaha Ave.

3rd St.

State Capitol

7th St.

Kellogg Blvd.

Indian Mounds Reg Park

McKnight Rd.

City Hall

Sam Morgan Reg Trail

Upper Afton Rd.

94

Battle Creek Reg Trail

Harriet Island Reg Park

ST. PAUL

Lower Afton Rd.

George St.

Smith Ave.

Robert St.

52

Pig's Eye Reg Park

61

Burlington Rd.

Point Douglas Rd.

Match Line

0   ½   1   2
Miles

Highlights include the state capitol, St. Paul's
Cathedral and Summit Ave., with it's 19th
century fine homes. The route leads back to
the Mississippi River and the starting point via
Edgecombe Road and Highland Park.

Cedar Lake Trail

Trail Length	5.0 miles
Surface	Paved
Uses	Leisure bicycling, cross-county skiing, hiking
Location & Setting	This 5 mile paved trail is located in Minneapolis, with a separate parallel trail for foot traffic. Most services are available within a short distance. East Trailhead is accessed at Glenwood and 12th.
Information	Three Rivers Park District 763-559-9000
County	Hennepin

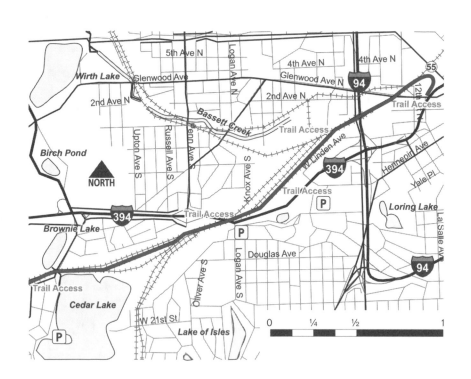

Fort Snelling State Park

Trail Length	5.0 miles
Surface	Paved
Uses	Leisure bicycling, inline skating, hiking
Location & Setting	Fort Snelling is located at the confluence of the Mississippi and Minnesota Rivers, just south of the twin cities. The trail is paved and parallels the two Rivers. Park entrance is off Hwy 5 at Post Road near the Minneapolis-St. Paul Airport.
Information	Fort Snelling State Park 612-727-1961
County	Dakota

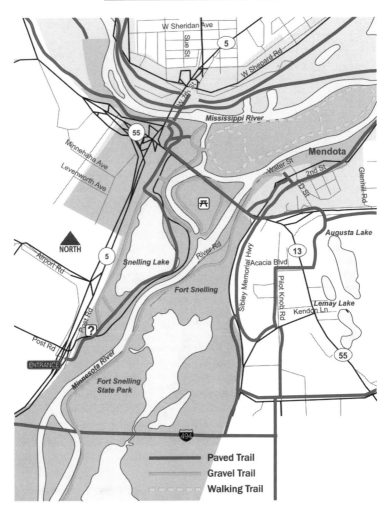

Lilydale Park Trail

Trail Length	7.0 miles
Surface	Asphalt
Uses	Leisure bicycling, hiking, in-line skating
Location & Setting	This trail runs from the 35E bridge to the LaFayette Bridge in downtown St. Paul. The bluffs on the west bank along the Big River Trail provide excellent views of the Mississippi. The trail on the east side of the river passes through the Hidden Falls area, paralleling Shepard Road into downtown St. Paul.
Information	St. Paul Parks Dept. 651-266-6400
County	Ramsey

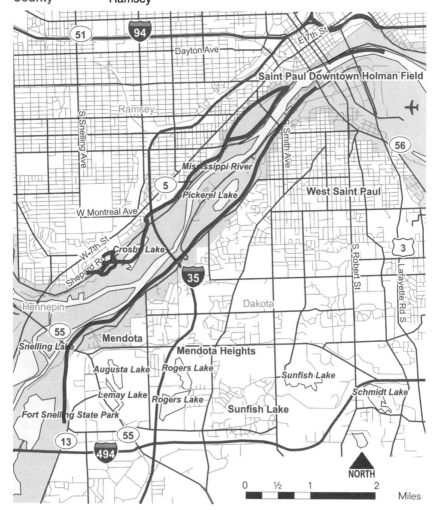

58

Midtown Greenway

Trail Length	5.5 miles
Surface	Paved
Uses	Leisure bicycling, in-line skating, jogging
Location & Setting	The Midtown Greenway is a long narrow park built all the way across Minneapolis along the 29th Street railroad corridor. The Greenway will include community gardens, play area, nature area, and bordering businesses and housing.
Information	Midtown Greenway Coalition 612-879-0103
Counties	Hennepin

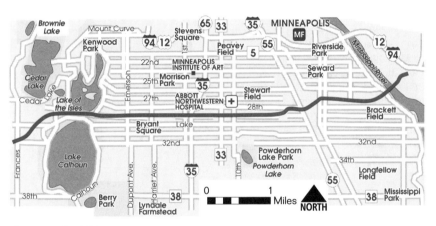

Because the Midtown Greenway is down below street level, bicyclists will be able to travel nonstop as they pass under bridges carrying the city street overhead. The Greenway will be lit at night and plowed in the winter. It will also link up with other planned bikeways connecting with St. Paul to the east and suburbs to the west.

SYMBOL LEGEND

🏖 Beach/Swimming		MF	Multi-Facilities
🚲 Bicycle Repair		P	Parking
🏠 Cabin		🎪	Picnic
⛺ Camping		🔺	Ranger Station
🛶 Canoe Launch		🚻	Restrooms
➕ First Aid		🏠	Shelter
🍴 Food		T	Trailhead
GC Golf Course		🏢	Visitor Center
❓ Information		🚰	Water
🛏 Lodging		🔭	Overlook/ Observation

St. Anthony Falls

Trail Length	1.8 miles, plus connecting streets
Surface	Asphalt
Uses	Leisure bicycling, in-line skating, jogging
Location & Setting	Straddles the Mississippi River between Stone Arch Bridge and Plymouth Avenue in north central Minneapolis. Level and easy with great views of Saint Anthony Falls and the Minneapolis skyline.
Information	Minneapolis Park & Recreation Board 612-661-9800
Counties	Hennepin

The bikeway over Stone Arch Bridge provides a spectacular view of the Falls. It was these Falls that allowed Minneapolis to lead the world in milling from 1880 to 1930 with the flour mills that sprang up along the river banks.

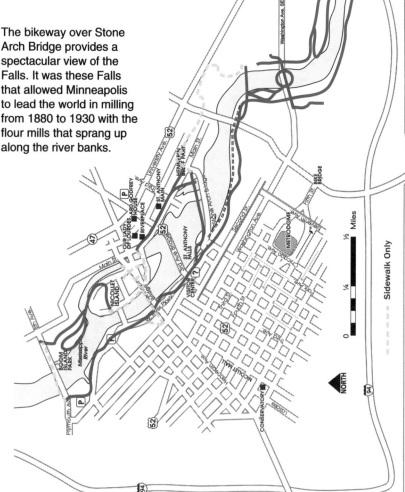

Theodore Wirth Park

Trail Length	3.4 miles
Surface	Natural
Uses	Mountain bicycling, cross-country skiing, hiking
Location & Setting	Theodore Wirth Park straddles Theo Wirth Parkway, stretching from Hwy 394 north to Golden Valley Road, bordering Minneapolis and Golden Valley. The bike trails are located just west of the Parkway and north of Hwy 55. The trails run generally clockwise and are one-way as it twists and climbs. Effort level is easy to moderate plus a few difficult alternatives. This scenic 500 acre park surrounds Wirth Lake. It has a swimming beach and the Eloise Butler Wildflower Garden is nearby. The parking lot is off Glenwood Avenue on the south side of Wirth Lake, or you can bike there via a paved trail running adjacent to the Parkway, which connects to paved trails around Cedar Lake, Lake Calhoun, and the other paved trails in the Minneapolis bike trail system.
Information	Theodore Wirth Park 763-522-4584
Counties	Hennepin

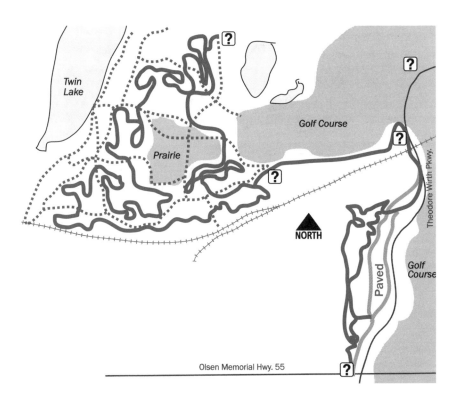

West Metro

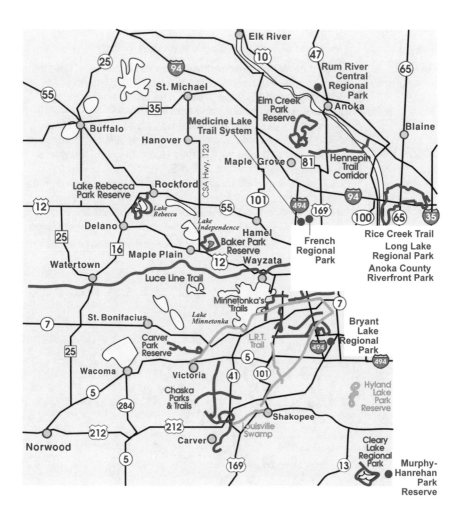

West Metro Trails   **Page**

Three Rivers Park District

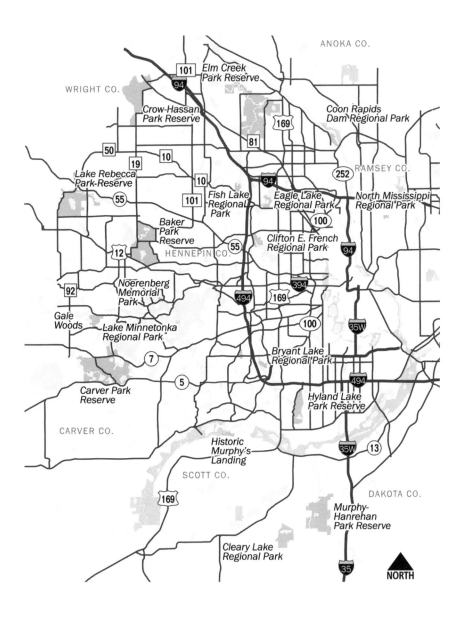

The Three Rivers Park District, formerly Hennepin Parks, is located in the suburban Minneapolis/St. Paul metro area. It consists of nearly 27,000 acres of park reserves, regional parks, regional trails and special-use facilities. Each is located within watersheds that flow into three rivers – the Mississippi, Minnesota, and Crow.

General Park Hours
Open 5 a.m. to sunset.

Visitors Centers
Cleary Lake
6:30 am to 9 pm daily June & July; 7 am to 8pm daily August

French & Hyland Park
9 am to 9 pm daily, June & July; 9 am to 8 pm daily August
Mountain bike trails close for the season on October 31

Baker Park Reserve
Winter Mountain Biking available as snow conditions permit. Mountain biking is not allowed in the spring, summer or fall.

Murphy-Hanrehan Park Reserve
Sunrise to Sunset as conditions permit. Special-use permit required.

Elm Creek Park Reserve

Lake Rebecca Park Reserve

Coon Rapid Dam Regional Park
Sunrise to Sunset as conditions permit.

Three Rivers Park District Maps included in this publication:

Three Rivers Park District
Baker Park Reserve

Trail Length	8.2 miles
Surface	Asphalt
Uses	Leisure bicycling, cross country skiing, in-line skating, jogging
Location & Setting	Located approximately 20 miles west of downtown Minneapolis on County Rd. 19, between Hwy. 12 and 55. Rolling hills, scenic views.
Information	Three Rivers Park District 763-559-9070
County	Hennepin

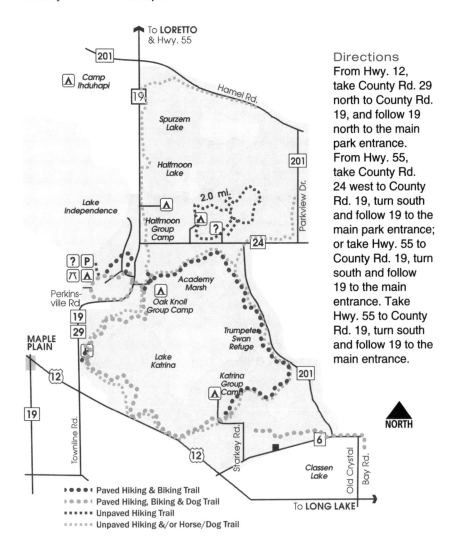

Directions
From Hwy. 12, take County Rd. 29 north to County Rd. 19, and follow 19 north to the main park entrance. From Hwy. 55, take County Rd. 24 west to County Rd. 19, turn south and follow 19 to the main park entrance; or take Hwy. 55 to County Rd. 19, turn south and follow 19 to the main entrance. Take Hwy. 55 to County Rd. 19, turn south and follow 19 to the main entrance.

To LORETTO & Hwy. 55

Camp Ihduhapi

Hamel Rd.

Spurzem Lake

Halfmoon Lake

2.0 mi.

Lake Independence

Halfmoon Group Camp

Perkinsville Rd

MAPLE PLAIN

Academy Marsh

Oak Knoll Group Camp

Trumpeter Swan Refuge

Lake Katrina

Katrina Group Camp

Parkview Dr.

Townline Rd.

Starkey Rd.

Classen Lake

Old Crystal Bay Rd.

To LONG LAKE

NORTH

- ● ● ● ● ● Paved Hiking & Biking Trail
- ◦ ◦ ◦ ◦ Paved Hiking, Biking & Dog Trail
- ■ ■ ■ ■ ■ Unpaved Hiking Trail
- ░ ░ ░ ░ Unpaved Hiking &/or Horse/Dog Trail

Three Rivers Park District
Bryant Lake
Regional Park

Trail Length	2 miles
Surface	Paved
Uses	Leisure bicycling, cross-country skiing, in-line skating, hiking
Location & Setting	Bryant Lake Regional Park is located in Eden Prairie, and has an area of 170 acres. In addition to bicycling and hiking, the park features a swimming beach on Bryant Lake Disc Golf. From Hwy 212, take Route 61 (Shady Oak Road) north to Rowland Road, then left (west) to the park entrance.
Information	Bryant Lake Regional Park 763-694-7764
County	Hennepin

Bunker Hills Regional Park

Trail Length	6.0 miles
Surface	Paved
Uses	Leisure bicycling, hiking, in-line skating, cross-country skiing, horseback riding
Location & Setting	This 1,600 acre park is located at the north side of Coon Rapids, a suburb of the twin cities. Surface is paved. Recreation facilities include swimming, camping, picnicking, horseback riding and a Wave Pool. Access from the south is on CR 4 off Main St. east of Hanson Blvd. Access from the north on CR A, off Bunker Lake Blvd.
Information	Anoka County Parks 763-757-3920
County	Anoka

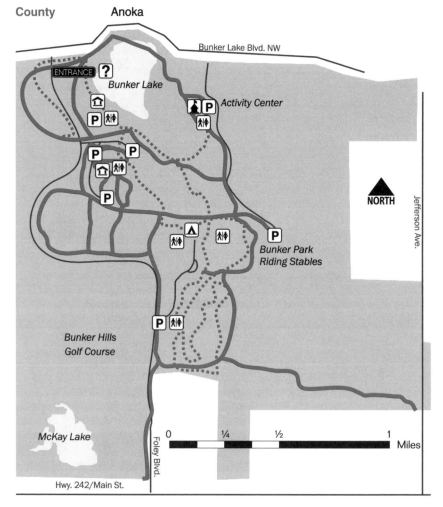

Three Rivers Park District
Carver Park Reserve

Trail Length	8.5 miles
Surface	Asphalt
Uses	Leisure bicycling, cross country skiing, in-line skating, jogging
Location & Setting	Located in Victoria, on Carver County Road 11. Take Highway 7 west from Minneapolis and turn left on County Road 11 or take Highway 5 west from Minneapolis and turn right on County Road 11. Follow signs to picnic area or trailhead. Moderate terrain. Rest stops at Lowry Nature Center and Parley Lake picnic area. Access from Nature Center or picnic area.
Information	Three Lakes Park District 763-559-9070
County	Carver

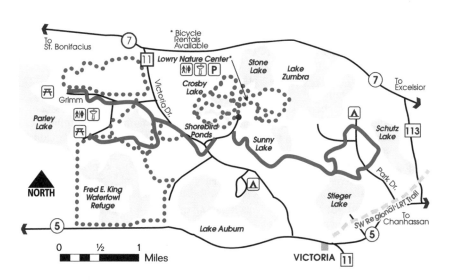

Additional short turf trails near Nature Center. The Minnesota Landscape Arboretum is nearby and allows biking on a three mile drive.

Paved bike trails connects to the 27 miles Southwest Regional LRT Trail via an aggregate connector trail running parallel to Park Drive.

Chaska's Trails

Trail Length	20.0 miles
Surface	Paved, gravel*
Uses	Leisure bicycling, cross country skiing, in-line skating, hiking
Location & Setting	Chaska is located in Carver County, southwest of the Twin Cities. The City Square is a good place to start, but there are numerous access points with parking along the route. You'll travel past lakes, through wooded ravines, experiencing some hills in addition to suburban areas.
Information	City of Chaska 952-448-2851
County	Carver

The path between Chaska City Square and Shakopee is paved. The route along Pioneer Trail Road is a paved shoulder. The remainder of the route is mostly gravel.

Nearby Area Attractions

Lowry Nature Center Box 270, Victoria, MN 55386
Open year round. Tues.-Sat. 9am-5pm, Sun noon-5pm; also open Memorial Day-Labor Day: Mon 9am-5pm. This park has 4 large lakes, camping, canoeing, hiking, biking and horseback riding trails, recreation play area, bird feeding station, 4 observation decks and a half-mile floating dock in the marsh. Also, beehive observation, family programs and bike rental. Informational displays, self guided trail brochures. Hennepin park permit required, with a daily or annual fee. Free parking available the first Tues. of each month. Located 8.5 mi W of Excelsior on Co Rd 11. Also 6 mi W of Chanhassen on Hwy 5, then 1.5 mi N on CR 11.
Scott County Historical Society 235 S Fuller St, Shakopee, MN 55379 • Open year round. Wed-Sat 10am-4pm. This museum contains African art and artifacts as well as local history. Donations appreciated. Free parking. 1 blk N of Court House in Shakopee.
Historic Murphy's Landing 2187 East Hwy 101, Shakopee, MN 55379
Mar-Dec. Memorial Day-Labor Day: T-Sun 10am-5pm; Mar-Dec: M-F by reservation; Thanksgiving-Christmas: Sat & Sun 10am-4pm. Living history re-creation of 1840-90 settler life; fur trader cabin, farms, blacksmith, town square, shops; boat excursion, schoolhouse classes, costumed interpreters, horse drawn trolley, restaurant, gift shop; located on 87 acres in the Minnesota River Valley. Admission fee, with group rate available. Free parking. Located 1 mile east of Shakopee on Hwy 101.

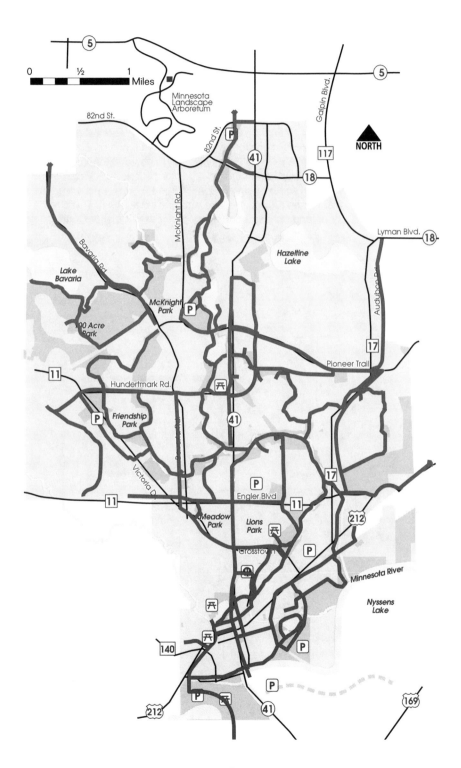

Three Rivers Park District
Cleary Lake Regional Park

Trail Length	3.5 miles
Surface	Asphalt
Uses	Leisure bicycling, cross country skiing, in-line skating, jogging
Location & Setting	Near Prior Lake on Scott County Road 27. From Highway 35W, go west on County Road 42, then south on County Road 27, or take I-494 to County Road 18, go south on 18, then east on Highway 101, south on Highway 13, east on County Road 42, then south again on County Road 27 to the park entrance. Flat terrain around the lake with one gradual hill. Three rest stops and one water pump stop. Access at Visitor Center.
Information	Cleary Lake Visitor Center 763-694-7777
County	Scott

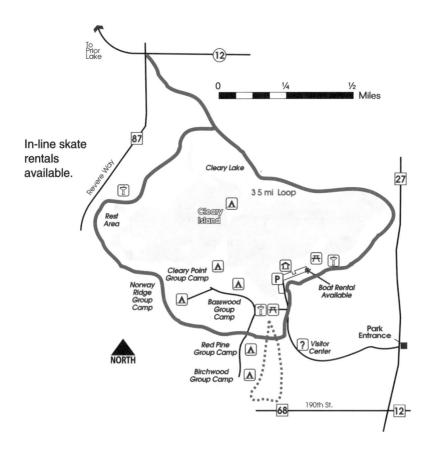

72

Three Rivers Park District
Coon Rapids Dam Regional Park

Trail Length	3.0 miles
Surface	Asphalt
Uses	Leisure bicycling, hiking, in-line skating, cross-country skiing
Location & Setting	This 3 mile trail is surfaced with asphalt and is 8 feet wide. It's located in Anoka County and connects with the North Hennepin Regional Trail in the north and the Mississippi River Regional Trail to the south. Bicycle rentals, restroom, and picnic facilities are available.
Information	Three Rivers Park District 763-559-9070 Coon Rapids Damp Visitors Center 763-757-4700
County	Anoka

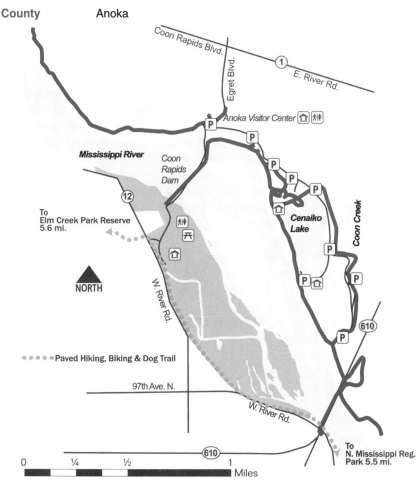

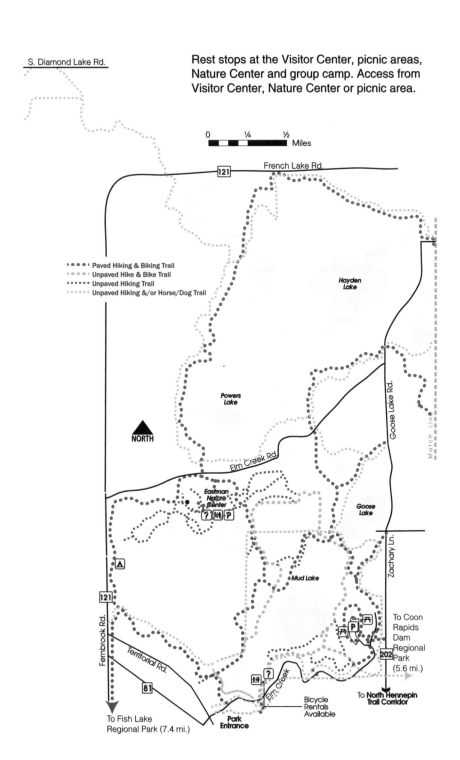

Rest stops at the Visitor Center, picnic areas, Nature Center and group camp. Access from Visitor Center, Nature Center or picnic area.

S. Diamond Lake Rd.

0   ¼   ½   Miles

French Lake Rd.

121

● ● ● ● Paved Hiking & Biking Trail
○ ○ ○ Unpaved Hike & Bike Trail
■ ■ ■ ■ Unpaved Hiking Trail
∴ ∴ ∴ Unpaved Hiking &/or Horse/Dog Trail

Hayden Lake

Powers Lake

NORTH

Goose Lake Rd.

Elm Creek Rd.

Eastman Nature Center

? 👥 P

Goose Lake

Match Line

Zachary Ln.

Mud Lake

To Coon Rapids Dam Regional Park (5.6 mi.)

202

🏕

121

Fernbrook Rd.

P 🏕

P

👥 ?

Elm Creek

To North Hennepin Trail Corridor

Territorial Rd.

81

Bicycle Rentals Available

To Fish Lake Regional Park (7.4 mi.)

Park Entrance

Three Rivers Park District
Elm Creek Park Reserve

Trail Length	Paved Trails 20.0 miles Mountain Bike Trails 4.4 miles	
Surface	Asphalt	
Uses	Leisure bicycling, cross country skiing, in-line skating, jogging	
Location & Setting	Located northwest of Osseo, between the communities of Champlin, Dayton and Maple Grove. Take County Rd. 81 northwest to Territorial Rd. Turn right and follow to the park entrance. Hilly terrain. Trail connects with North Hennepin Trail Corridor.	
Information	Three Rivers Park District 763-559-9070 Elm Creek Visitors Center 763-694-7894	
County	Hennepin	

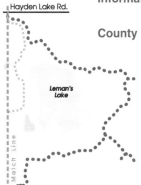

Hayden Lake Rd.

Leman's Lake

Match Line

SYMBOL LEGEND

🏖	Beach/Swimming	MF	Multi-Facilities
🚲	Bicycle Repair	P	Parking
🏠	Cabin	🏕	Picnic
A	Camping	🏠	Ranger Station
🛶	Canoe Launch	🚻	Restrooms
+	First Aid	🏠	Shelter
🍴	Food	T	Trailhead
GC	Golf Course	🏛	Visitor Center
?	Information	💧	Water
🛏	Lodging	🔭	Overlook/ Observation

Nearby Area Attractions

Ellingson Car Museum 20950 Rogers Drive, Rogers, MN 55374
Open year round. Monday-Saturday 10am-6pm; Sunday noon-5pm;
closed Thanksgiving, Christmas, New Year's Day, Easter. Over 90
different cars, trucks and motorcycles set up by decade, historic videos
and memorabilia accompany each display; displays include WWII tank,
rendition of 1950s drive-in movie with old film clips, speed shop, replica
of 1060s drag strip. Kids 12 and under admitted free. Exit Hwy 101
from I-94.

Three Rivers Park District
French Regional Park

Trail Length	3.4 miles
Surface	Paved
Uses	Leisure bicycling, cross-country skiing, in-line skating, hiking
Location & Setting	This 310 acre park is located on the north shore of Medicine Lake in Plymouth. Paved trails lead from the park entrance to the visitor center, play area, beach and through maple woodlands. They connect to the regional trail along the lake's east shore and will lead you to the Luce Line State Trail. The trails are lighted. From I-494, take County Road 9 (Rockford Road) east 1 mile to the park entrance.
Information	French Regional Park Visitor Center 763-694-7750
County	Hennepin

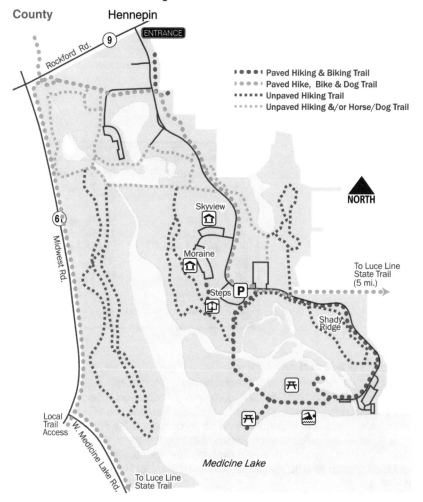

Legend:
- ●●●● Paved Hiking & Biking Trail
- ○●○● Paved Hike, Bike & Dog Trail
- ▪▪▪▪▪ Unpaved Hiking Trail
- ░░░░░ Unpaved Hiking &/or Horse/Dog Trail

Hennepin Trail Corridor

Trail Length	7.2 miles
Surface	Asphalt
Uses	Leisure bicycling, in-line skating, jogging
Location & Setting	Connects the Coon Rapids Dam Regional Park to Elm Creek Park Reserve. Coon Rapids Park is located on the Mississippi River in Brooklyn Park. From Highway 252, turn west on County Rd. 30, then take County Rd. 12 north to park entrance. Relatively flat terrain.
Information	Hennepin Parks Trail Corridor 768-559-9000
County	Hennepin

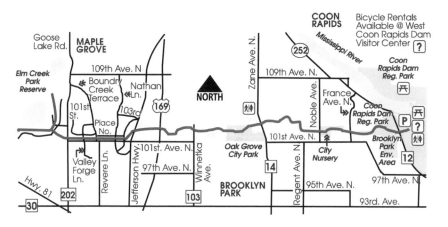

In-line skate and bike rentals available at West Coon Rapids Dam Visitor Center.

In addition to the biking trail, the Trail Corridor has a parallel multi-use trail open to horseback riding, snowmobiling and cross country skiing.

Nearby Area Attractions

Brooklyn Park Historical Farm
4345 101st Ave N, Brooklyn Park, MN 55443
May-Aug: Wed. & Sun. noon - 4 pm. Depiction of rural Minnesota at the turn of the century, guided tours of restored farmstead, hands-on activities, living history events in the fall. $.50-$3. Free parking. I-94 North or I-694 to 252, North to 93rd Ave. North (4.1 mi), West to Regent Avenue North (2.1mi), North to 101st Ave North (1mi), East to 4345 101st Ave. North (.5 mi).

Hyland Lake Park Reserve

Trail Length	8.6 miles
Surface	Asphalt
Uses	Leisure bicycling, cross country skiing, in-line skating, jogging
Location & Setting	Located on East Bush Lake Road in Bloomington. From I-494, go south on Normandale Boulevard to 84th Street. Turn Right and follow 84th Street to East Bush Lake Road. Go south on East Lake Bush Road and follow the signs to Richardson Nature Center and Hyland Lake Visitor Center. The northern loop takes you through rolling hills and scenic meadows, while the southern travels through woodlands. Trails connect to adjacent neighborhoods. Two rest areas. Access from Visitor Center.
Information	Hyland Lake Park Reserve 763-694-7687
County	Hennepin

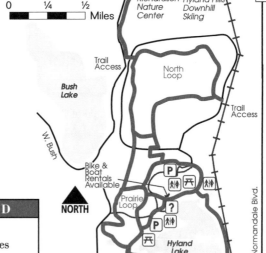

0   ¼   ½
Miles

TRAIL LEGEND

— Bike Trail
▭▭▭ Bicycle Lanes
· · · · · Hiking only Trail
• • • • • Multi Use Trail
▬▬▬ Snowmobiling only
= = = = Planned Trail
– – – – Alternate Trail
— Road/Highway
+++++++ Railroad Tracks

Three Rivers Park District
Lake Rebecca
Park Reserve

Trail Length	7.0 miles
Surface	Asphalt
Uses	Leisure & mountain bicycling, cross-country skiing, in-line skating, jogging
Location & Setting	Located approximately 30 miles west of Minneapolis on County Road 50. Take Highway 55 west to County Road 50, turn left and follow to the park entrance. Hilly trail through scenic, wooded terrain. Two rest stops; water available in picnic area. Access from recreation/picnic area parking lot.
Information	Lake Rebecca Park Reserve 763-694-7860
County	Hennepin

Minnesota Valley State Recreation Area
Louisville Swamp

Trail Length	6.5 miles
Surface	Paved (plus 13.5 miles grass & dirt trail)
Uses	Leisure bicycling, in-line skating, cross country skiing, hiking
Location & Setting	Southwest of Minneapolis with trailheads in Shakopee and Chaska. There is parking in Chaska off State Highway 41 and in Shakopee at the Huber Park trailhead near city hall, one block east of Highway 169. The trail was built on an old railroad bed. It crosses the Minnesota River on the original railroad swing bridge.
Information	Minnesota Valley State Park 952-492-6400
County	Carver

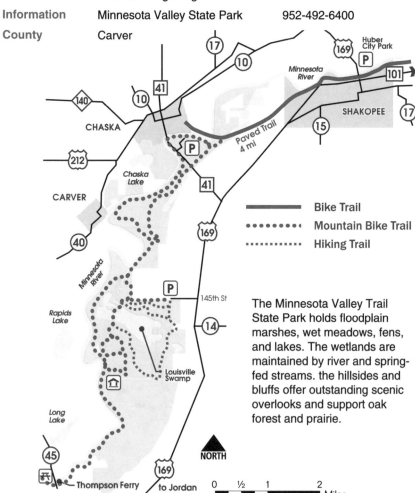

Bike Trail

Mountain Bike Trail

Hiking Trail

The Minnesota Valley Trail State Park holds floodplain marshes, wet meadows, fens, and lakes. The wetlands are maintained by river and spring-fed streams. the hillsides and bluffs offer outstanding scenic overlooks and support oak forest and prairie.

Three Rivers Park District
LRT Trail

Trail Length	North corridor - 15.5 miles South corridor - 11.5 miles
Surface	Crushed limestone - 10 feet wide
Uses	Leisure bicycling, cross country skiing, hiking
Location & Setting	The Southwest Regional LRT Trail includes two corridors that follow abandoned railroad right-of-way through the southwestern metro Twin Cities area. The north corridor begins in Hopkins on the west side of Eighth Avenue North, just north of Main street and runs to downtown Victoria. The south corridor also begins in Hopkins, at the Park and Ride lot southeast of the intersection of Eight Avenue South and County Road 3 and extends to Chanhassen.
Information	Three River Park District 763-559-9070
Counties	Hennepin, Carver

(See map on following pages)

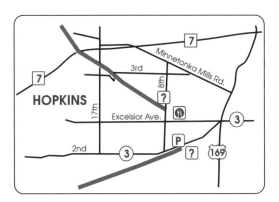

The Trails are two-way and includes wooden bridges and several road crossings. Designated parking areas are available along both corridors. Trail hours are from 5 a.m. to sunset. Motorized vehicles are prohibited.

The Hennepin Parks system consists of 25,000 acres of park land including seven large park reserves, five regional park Noerenberg Gardens, the North Hennepin Regional Trail Corridor besides the LRT trail.

The average trail grade is 1%, with a maximum of 5%. The average cross slope is 0% with a maximum of 1%.

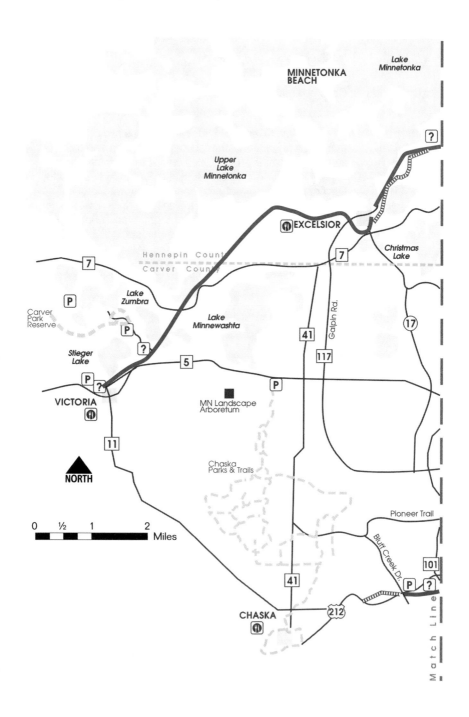

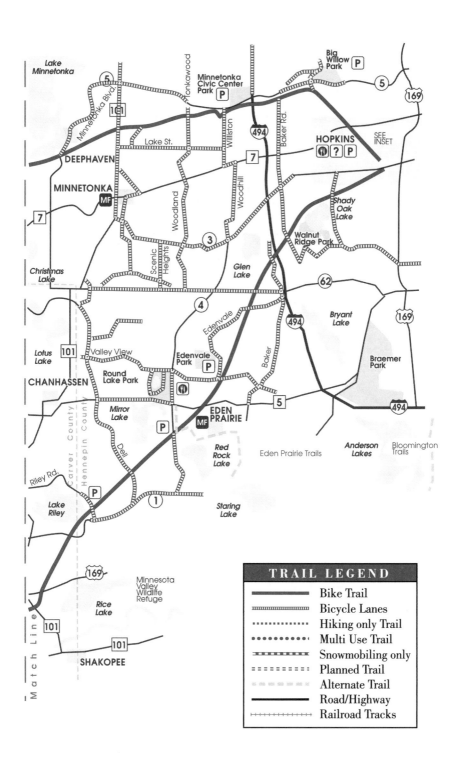

TRAIL LEGEND

▬▬▬▬	Bike Trail
▭▭▭▭	Bicycle Lanes
· · · · ·	Hiking only Trail
● ● ● ●	Multi Use Trail
▬▪▬▪▬	Snowmobiling only
= = = =	Planned Trail
▬ ▬ ▬	Alternate Trail
▬▬▬	Road/Highway
+++++	Railroad Tracks

83

Luce Line State Trail

Trail Length	66 miles: east segment 29.5 miles, west segment 31.5 miles
Surface	Limestone screenings - east segment Natural groomed - west segment
Uses	Leisure & fat tire bicycling, cross country skiing, snowmobiling, hiking, horseback riding
Location & Setting	The eastern trailhead is located in Plymouth, just west of Minneapolis, and continues for 64 miles to Thompson Lake, west of Cosmos The Luce Line State Trail was developed on an abandoned railroad line. The setting is open country with only scattered tree cover except for woodlands and more urban surroundings near the eastern end.
Information	Luce Line Trail Office 952-475-0371
Counties	Hennepin, Carver, McLeod, Meeker

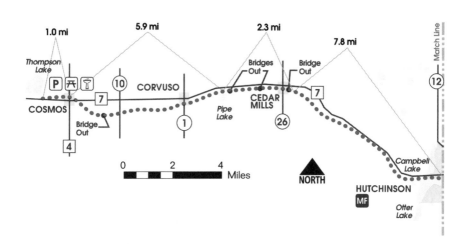

AREA OVERVIEW

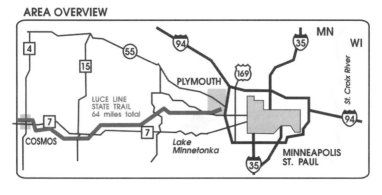

84

HUTCHINSON

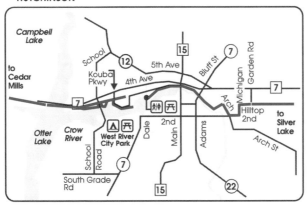

Limestone surface continues to County Rd. 9, 1 mile west of parking area. You can continue to Hutchinson via County Rd. 9 (south) and then west on State HWY 7. The trail continues from HWY 9 on County Route 85 (235th Street). Restaurants, restrooms, picnic, and lodging available.

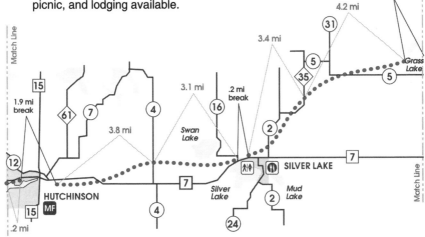

The .2 mile trail detour through Silver Lake is marked by signs. Restrooms, restaurant available in Silver Lake.

Trail detour of 1.9 miles begins just east of Hutchinson and is marked by signs. All normal services are available. West River City Park offers a campground and picnic area.

TRAIL LEGEND	
━━━━━━	Bike Trail
▭▭▭▭▭▭	Bicycle Lanes
··············	Hiking only Trail
●●●●●●●●●	Multi Use Trail
▰▰▰▰▰▰▰	Snowmobiling only
=========	Planned Trail
▭ ▭ ▭ ▭ ▭	Alternate Trail
━━━━━━	Road/Highway
┼┼┼┼┼┼┼┼┼	Railroad Tracks

85

AREA LEGEND

- ▨ City, Town
- ▨ Parks, Preserves
- ▢ Waterway
- ▨ Marsh/Wetland
- ▬▬ Mileage Scale
- ★ Points of Interest
- –– County/State
- 🌲 Forest/Woods

ROUTE SLIP	INCREMENT	TOTAL	ELEV.
Plymouth			1000
Vicksburg Ln.	1.1	1.1	
Old Long Lake Rd.	2.9	4.0	
Orono (Willow Dr.)	2.5	6.5	
Stubbs Bay	1.3	7.8	935
County Rd. 110	2.4	10.2	
Lyndale	3.4	13.6	
HWY 127	2.5	16.1	
Watertown (HWY 10)	3.5	19.6	960
HWY 21	4.5	24.1	
HWY 33	2.0	26.1	
Winsted	3.4	29.5	1010
Trail Break	*1.4*		
HWY 35	4.2	33.7	
Silver Lake (HWY 2)	3.4	37.1	1050
HWY 4	3.1	40.2	
Hutchinson	3.8	44.0	1056
Trail Break	*1.9*		
Cedar Mills	8.0	52.0	
Pipe Lake	2.3	54.3	
Cosmos	5.9	60.2	1112
Thompson Lake	1.0	61.2	

WATERTOWN

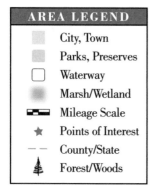

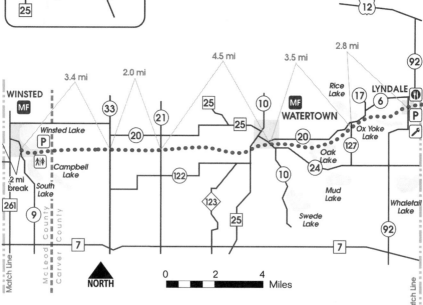

Parking, restrooms, and restaurants near the Watertown trailheads.

SYMBOL LEGEND

🏖	Beach/Swimming	MF	Multi-Facilities
🚲	Bicycle Repair	P	Parking
🏠	Cabin	🛆	Picnic
▲	Camping	🛆	Ranger Station
🛶	Canoe Launch	🚻	Restrooms
+	First Aid	⌂	Shelter
🍴	Food	T	Trailhead
GC	Golf Course	🏛	Visitor Center
?	Information	🚰	Water
🛏	Lodging	🔭	Overlook/ Observation

PLYMOUTH TRAILHEAD

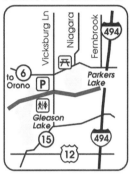

The city of Plymouth has a 1.1 mile paved spur west to I-494.

East Trailhead

From I-494 exit west on HWY 12 (Wayzata Blvd.) to County Rd. 15 (Gleason Lake Rd.) Turn north and exit to the north on Vicksburg Lane. Continue north to 10th Ave. N. (note sign) and turn west a half block to the parking lot. Restrooms and picnic area available. If you are traveling west on HWY 55, west of I-494, turn south on Vicksburg Lane.

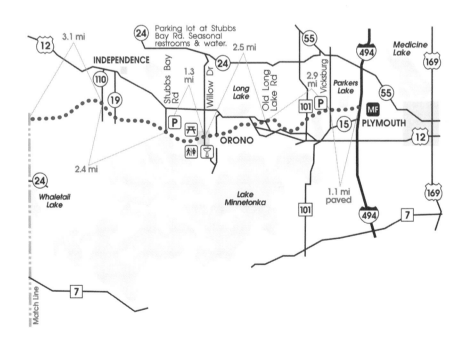

Medicine Lake Trail System

Trail Length	5 to 15 miles
Surface	Paved, crushed limestone
Uses	Leisure bicycling, in-line skating, cross country skiing, hiking
Location & Setting	The paved trail around Medicine Lake is wide and smooth, providing enjoyable riding for visitors of all ages. Facilities include beaches, picnic area, comfort benches and well-spaced toilets. There are two long wooden bridges that meander through the marshlands with widened sections for scenic viewing. There is also an historic covered wooden bridge located in the West Park.
Information	Three River Park District 763-559-9000
Counties	Hennepin

Clifton E. French Regional Park
Add to your ride with a 1 mile track inside Clifton E. French Regional Park. The park offers food, beaches, playground and well-maintained grounds for your visiting pleasure.

Linking Up
For a long ride, take the 3 Rivers Park spur that leads to the Luce Line Trail, 4 miles from Medicine Lake West Park to the trailhead. The spur is paved. It takes you through woods, past several ponds and under two major highways. There are rest benches along the way.

Ride Mileage	Miles
West Medicine Lake Park around the lake to the back entrance of French Park	4.3
Additional ride within French Park	1.0
Round trip back to the starting point	8.0
To the Luce Line trailhead – add	4.0
To Orono – add	6.0
To Baker Regional Park & inside – add	6.0

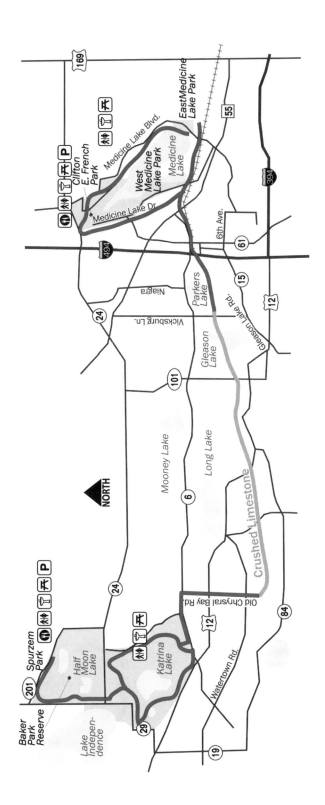

NORTH

169

EastMedicine
Lake Park

Medicine Lake Blvd.

55

Clifton
E. French
Park

P

West
Medicine
Lake Park

Medicine
Lake

394

* Medicine Lake Dr

6th Ave.

494

61

Niagra

Parkers
Lake

15

24

Vicksburg Ln.

12

Gleason Lake Rd.

Gleason
Lake

101

Mooney Lake

Long Lake

6

Crushed Limestone

Spurzem
Park

P

Baker
Park
Reserve

201

Half
Moon
Lake

*

Old Chrystal Bay Rd.

84

24

Katrina
Lake

12

Watertown Rd.

Lake
Indepen-
dence

29

19

Minnetonka's Trails

Trail Length	40.0 miles
Surface	Asphalt, concrete or limestone screenings; 8 feet wide
Uses	Leisure bicycling, in-line skating, hiking
Location & Setting	Minnetonka is a community of approximately 50,000 located in the western metropolitan Twin-Cities area. The trail system connects all of Minnetonka's cultural and commercial activity centers as well as the Luce Line and Southwest Regional LRT Trails which transverse the city.
Information	Minnetonka Trails Hotline 932-738-7245
County	Hennepin

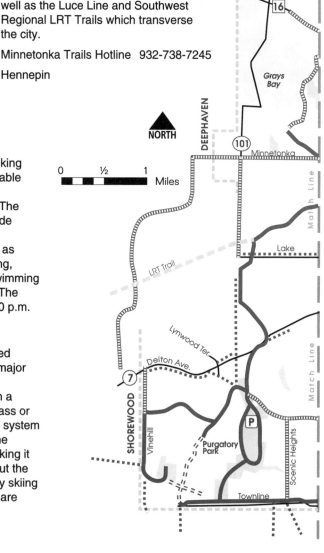

Restroom and drinking fountains are available in each of the five community parks. The park facilities include a wide variety of opportunities such as picnicking, canoeing, fishing, skating, swimming and group sports. The trails close at 10:00 p.m.

At most uncontrolled intersections with major roadways, the trail crosses the road in a pedestrian underpass or overpass. The trail system is plowed during the winter months, making it available throughout the year. Cross country skiing and snowmobiling are prohibited.

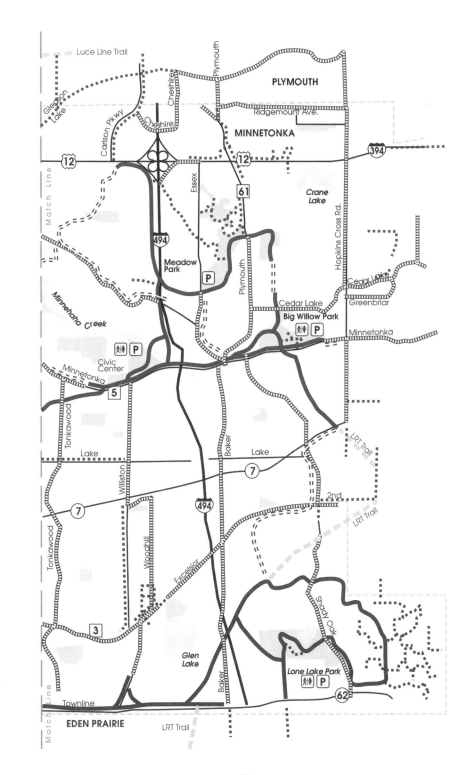

Three Rivers Park District
Murphy-Hanrehan
Park Reserve

Trail Length	6.0 miles
Surface	Natural
Uses	Mountain bicycling, hiking, horseback riding
Location & Setting	The glacial ridges and hilly terrain of northwest Scott County make this 2,400 acre park popular with mountain bikers, hikers, and cross-country skiers. The trail is well maintained. The terrain within the park is rugged with a number of steep hills. Grades are long and steep. The bicycle trail is open from sunrise to sunset, and is closed for the season at the end of October. There is a parking fee. The park is located near Prior Lake. From I-35W, take CR 42 (Eagan Dr) to CR 74 (Hanrehan Lake Blvd.), then south to CR 75 (Murphy Lake Blvd), continuing south to the Park entrance.
Information	Murphy-Hanrehan Park Reserve 952-447-6913
County	Scott

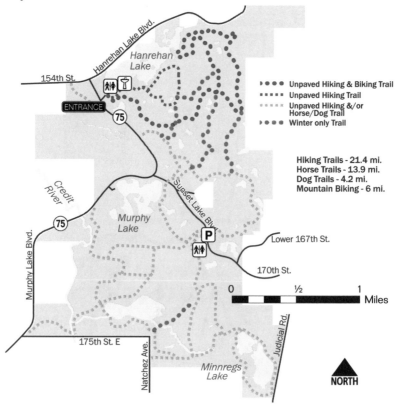

Unpaved Hiking & Biking Trail
Unpaved Hiking Trail
Unpaved Hiking &/or Horse/Dog Trail
Winter only Trail

Hiking Trails - 21.4 mi.
Horse Trails - 13.9 mi.
Dog Trails - 4.2 mi.
Mountain Biking - 6 mi.

NORTH

Rice Creek West Regional Trail
Long Lake Regional Park
Anoka County Riverfront Park

Trail Length	8.0 miles (18.0 miles loop with street routes)
Surface	Paved, gravel
Uses	Leisure bicycling, cross country skiing, in-line skating, jogging
Location & Setting	This path takes you from Long Lake in New Brighton west along Rice Creek through Findley and a ride along the Mississippi River through Anoka County Riverfront Park to 42nd Avenue. From the intersection of I-35W and I-694, take I-35W to Highway 96, then west to 1st Avenue, then south to the park entrance. Waterviews, parkways, urban.
Information	Long Lake Regional Park 651-698-4543 Anoka County Park 763-757-3920
Counties	Anoka, Ramsey

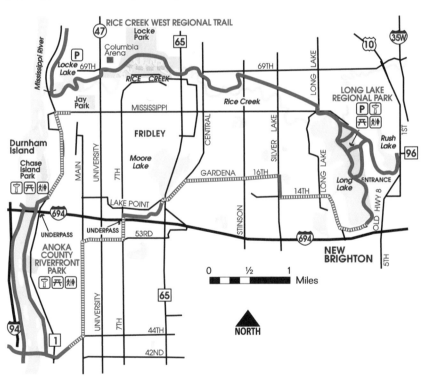

The route is mainly level except for some short grades and gravel paths along Rice Creek east of Central. There is a short road connection on Stinson, and another stretch with a wide bike lane along East River Rd.

Rum River Central Regional Park

Trail Length	3 miles
Surface	Paved
Uses	Leisure bicycling, cross-country skiing, in-line skating, hiking, horseback riding
Location & Setting	This 434 acre, scenic natural park is located on the Rum River. It features a diversity of river, prairie, and woodland settings covering 434 acres. Facilities include a boat/canoe launch, restrooms, picnic area, and canoe campsites. The entrance is off 179th Lane NW and can be accessed from County Road 47, three miles north of Hwy 10.
Information	Rum River Central Regional Park 763-757-3920
County	Anoka

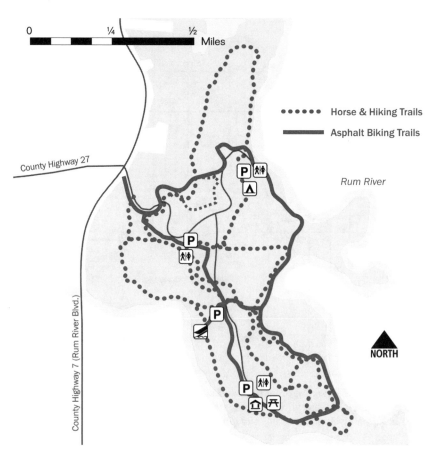

East Metro

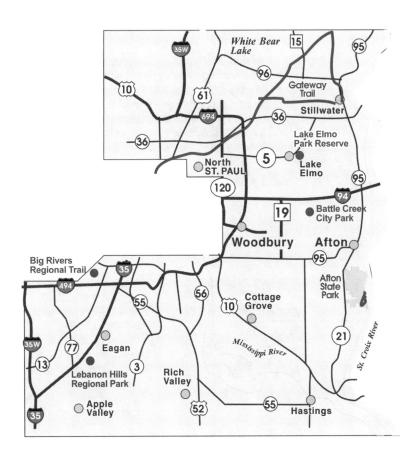

Afton State Park

Trail Length	4.0 miles
Surface	Asphalt
Uses	Leisure bicycling, cross country skiing, hiking
Location & Setting	Located less than an hour from the Twin Cities in Washington County. The 1,695 acre park entrance is off Highway 20, just east of Highway 21. Afton State Park lies on the bluffs overlooking the St. Croix River where it is cut by deep ravines. Outcrops of sandstone jut from the side of the ravines. The rugged terrain affords spectacular views of the St. Croix Valley. Above the forested ravines are rolling fields and pastures.
Information	Afton State Park Manager 651-436-5391
County	Washington

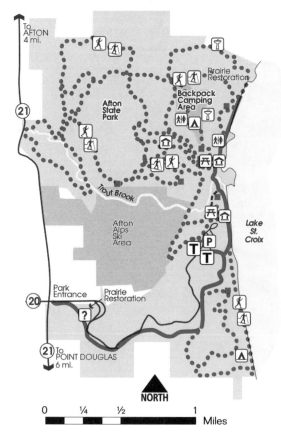

Afton State Park was established in 1969. The park offers opportunities for biking, hiking, cross country skiing, swimming, picnicking and camping. Wildlife includes fox, deer, badgers, hawks, eagles and warblers. In addition to biking, there are 18.0 miles of hiking and cross country ski trails and 5 miles of horseback riding trails. The Visitor Center facilities include interpretive, information and a pay telephone. The camp is closed from 10 pm to 8 am except for campers.

Big Rivers Regional Trail

Trail Length	4.5 miles
Surface	Asphalt
Uses	Leisure bicycling, cross-country skiing, in-line skating, hiking
Location & Setting	Situated along the northern edge of Dakota County, the Big Rivers Regional Trial provides a scenic 4.5-miles ride overlooking the confluence of the Minnesota and Mississippi Rivers and many historic landmarks including Fort Snelling and Pike Island as it parallels Hwy 13. The terrain is flat. Take I-35E to Mendota Heights. Exit on Hwy 13 (Sibley Memorial Hwy). Proceed west on Hwy 13 for 2 miles, then west on Sibley Memorial Hwy for 1.2 miles. Turn north (right) into the parking area and to the trailhead at stone overlook.
Information	Dakota County Parks Dept.　　　952-891-7000
County	Dakota

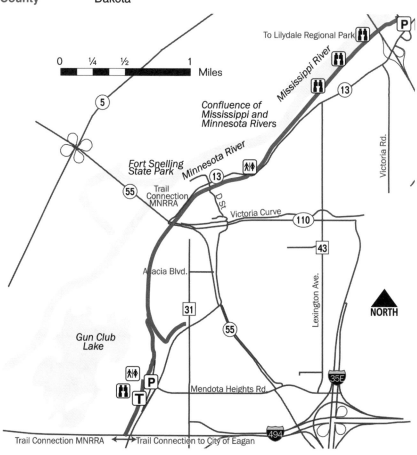

Gateway State Trail

Trail Length	18.0 miles
Surface	Paved
Uses	Leisure bicycling, in-line skating, cross country skiing, hiking/jogging
Location & Setting	The Gateway State Trail, a segment of the Willard Munger State Trail, is a paved, multi-use recreational trail starting 1 mile north of downtown St. Paul and continuing to Pine Point Park, 5 miles north of Stillwater. It cuts through a cross-section of urban area and parks, and extends out to lakes, wetlands, fields and wooded countryside.
Information	DNR Information Center 651-296-6157
Counties	Ramsey, Washington

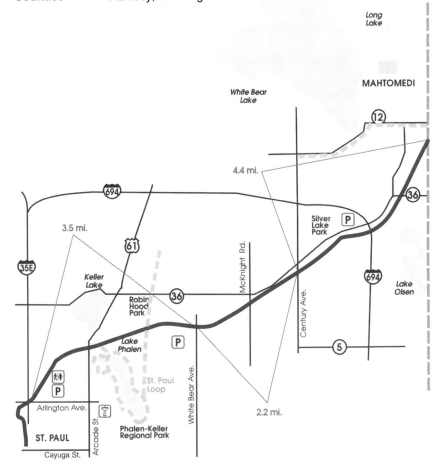

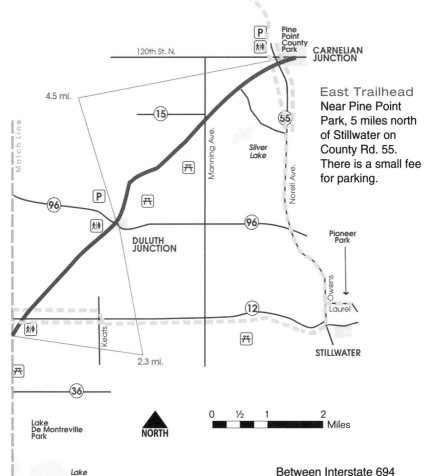

East Trailhead
Near Pine Point Park, 5 miles north of Stillwater on County Rd. 55. There is a small fee for parking.

West Trailhead Take the Larpenteur & Wheelock Parkway exit from Interstate 35E (3 miles north of downtown St. Paul). Go east 1 block to Westminister St. Turn right (south) and go 1/2 mile to Arlington Ave. Turn right (west) and go 1/2 block to the trail parking lot on the left (south) side of Arlington (near the Interstate 35E overpass).

Between Interstate 694 underpass and the east trailhead near Pine Point Park (9.7 miles) is a dual trailway: unpaved, for horseback riding and paved for biking.

Lebanon Hills Regional Park

Trail Length	4.5 miles
Surface	Natural
Uses	Fat tire biking, plus over 25-miles of designated trails for cross-country skiing, snowmobiling, horseback riding, and hiking.
Location & Setting	Lebanon Hills Regional Park, with over 2,000 acres, is located in Eagan and Apple Valley, in the heart of the southern Twin Cities Metropolitan area. The terrain is hilly with deep hardwoods, pristine lakes, marshes, and prairies. There are designated trails for each of the numerous uses. The park consists of a east and west section, with the mountain biking trail being located in the west section. Trail access is available off Galaxle Ave. or Johnny Cake Ridge Road. Location maps are posted at trail intersections along your route.
Information	Dakota County Parks Dept. 952-891-7000
County	Dakota

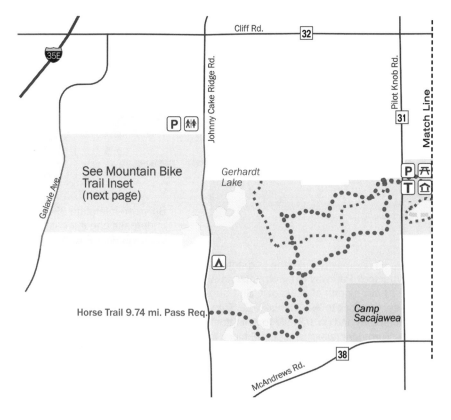

Campground **12100 Johnny Cake Ridge Road, Apple Valley.**
Jensen Trailhead **1350 Carriage Hills Drive, Eagan.**
Holland Trailhead **1100 Cliff Road, Eagan.**
Schulze Concession Stand **832 Cliff Road, Eagan.**
Visitor Center/Trailhead **836 Cliff Road, Eagan.**
Camp Sacajawea **5121 McAndrews Road, Apple Valley.**

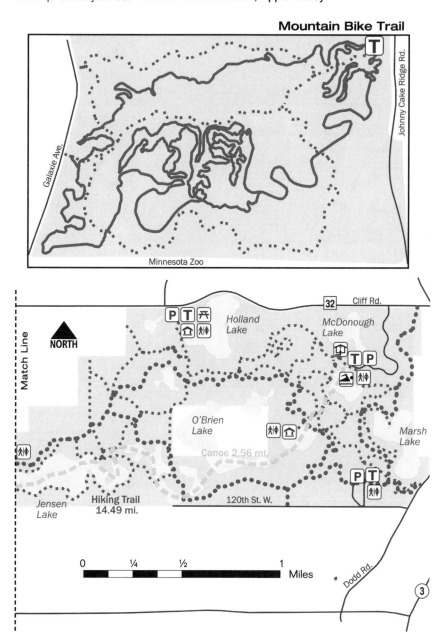

Northern Minnesota

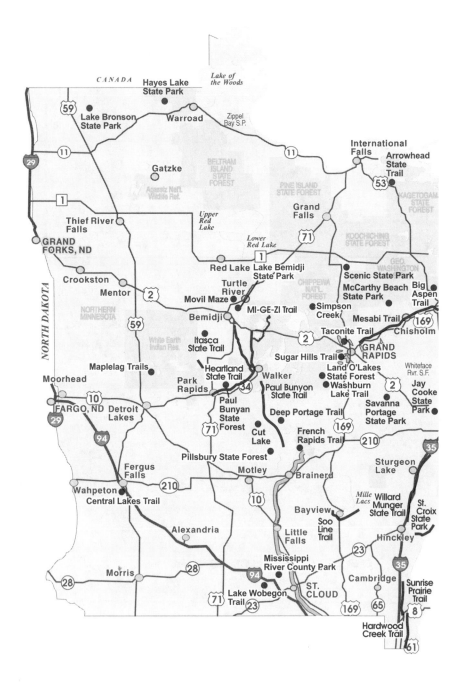

Arrowhead State Trail

Trail Length   135 miles

Surface   Natural

Uses   Mountain bicycling, cross-country skiing, horseback riding, snowmobiling

Location & Setting   Arrowhead State Trail is located in far northern Minnesota, and extends from the intersection with the Taconite State Trail near Tower to 3 miles south of International Falls. About 69 miles of the trail are suitable for mountain biking. The southern part of the trail features rolling hills with numerous lakes and streams. It is heavily timbered with a mix of hardwoods and conifers. The northern section of the trail is relatively flat between International Falls and the Ash River. It goes through a number of areas with standing water during the summer. The mix of trees on the Arrowhead is spectacularly colorful in autumn. Parking is available on Hwy 1, two miles west of Hwy 169.

Information   DNR Information Center   651-296-6157

Counties   St. Louis, Koochiching

The Arrowhead State Trail links
three state Parks: Bear Head
Lake, Soudan Underground Mine,
and McCarthy Beach. Soudan
Underground Mine State Park
is located on a rugged ridge
and contain the historic Soudan
underground mine. This is
Minnesota's only underground iron
ore mine open to the public.

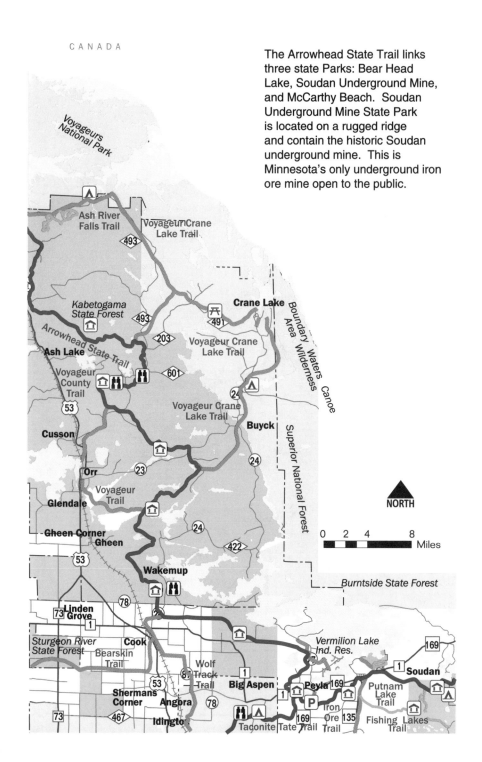

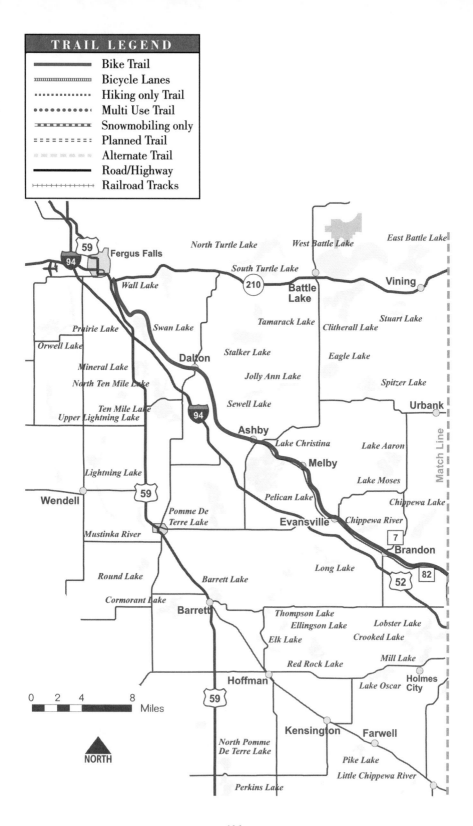

TRAIL LEGEND

————	Bike Trail
⊏⊏⊏⊏⊏⊏⊏	Bicycle Lanes
··············	Hiking only Trail
●●●●●●●●	Multi Use Trail
▬▬▬▬▬▬	Snowmobiling only
=========	Planned Trail
░░░░░░░	Alternate Trail
━━━━	Road/Highway
┼┼┼┼┼┼┼┼┼	Railroad Tracks

59
94
Fergus Falls

North Turtle Lake   West Battle Lake   East Battle Lake

South Turtle Lake   **210**   Vining
Wall Lake   Battle Lake

Prairie Lake   Swan Lake   Tamarack Lake   Clitherall Lake   Stuart Lake

Orwell Lake

Mineral Lake   Dalton   Stalker Lake   Eagle Lake

North Ten Mile Lake   Jolly Ann Lake   Spitzer Lake

Ten Mile Lake   **94**   Sewell Lake   Urbank
Upper Lightning Lake

Ashby   Lake Aaron
Lake Christina
Melby

Lightning Lake   Lake Moses

59   Chippewa Lake

Wendell   Pomme De   Pelican Lake   Chippewa River
Terre Lake

Mustinka River   Evansville   **7**
Brandon

Round Lake   Long Lake   **82**
Barrett Lake   **52**

Cormorant Lake   Barrett

Thompson Lake   Lobster Lake
Ellingson Lake
Elk Lake   Crooked Lake

Red Rock Lake   Mill Lake

Hoffman   Holmes
Lake Oscar   City
59

Kensington   Farwell

North Pomme
De Terre Lake   Pike Lake

Perkins Lake   Little Chippewa River

Match Line

0   2   4   8   Miles

NORTH

Central Lakes Trail

Trail Length	55.0 miles
Surface	Asphalt
Uses	Both leisure & fat tire bicycling, hiking, cross-country skiing
Location & Setting	This 55 mile, 14 foot wide trail was developed on old railbed and runs between Fergus Falls and Osakis, with a planned extension to Sauk Centre. The setting is rural and mostly open as it goes through farmland areas, and several communities in route. You will also pass by several picturesque lakes. Osakis and Alexandria are located off Interstate 94, less than 2.5 hours from the Twin Cities.
Information	Central Lakes Trail Office 320-763-6001
Counties	Douglas, Grant, Otter Tail, Stearns, Todd

Gitchi-Gami State Trail

Trail Length	86 miles planned with some 21 miles completed
Surface	Asphalt, undeveloped
Uses	Leisure bicycling, hiking, and cross-country skiing
Location & Setting	The Gitchi-Gami State Trail runs between Two Harbors and Grand Marais, along the north shore of Lake Superior, mostly on Hwy 61 right-of-way or on abandoned segment of Hwy 61. The trail will connect five state parks, several communities, and vistas of Lake Superior. It will travel through birch and aspen forest, and cross numerous cascades and waterfalls.
Information	DNR Information Center 651-296-6157
County	Cook

Available Parking

Silver Creek Segment At the Silver Creek wayside Rest Stop, located on the east side of the Silver Creek Cliff Tunnel.

Beaver Bay Segment At the trail center in Split Rock Lighthouse State Park, and the trailhead parking lot in Beaver Bay near the Beaver River.

Tofte Segment At the Tofte Town Park Public Access.

Grand Marais segment Near the public water access and the U.S. Coast Guard Station.

Cascade River State Park

Lutsen 61

Tofte

See Inset

Temperance River State Park

Schroeder

Taconite Harbor

George H. Crosby Manitou State Park

Lake Superior

61

Tettegouche State Park

Silver Bay
Beaver Bay

Split Rock Lighthouse State Park

See Inset

Gooseberry Falls State Park

Two Harbors

Completed segments as of this publication

Silver Creek Cliff Segment One mile on the old scenic Hwy 61 road be circumnavigating the Silver Creek Tunnel.

Gooseberry Falls State Park A total of 13.1 miles connecting Split Rock River and Beaver Bay, and Gooseberry Falls State Park to the Split Rock River. There is a spur connection to the historic Split Rock Lighthouse.

Temperance River State Park Segment This segment is 3.0 mile long and connects the town of Schroeder and Tofte. It travels through the interior of Temperance River State Park and crosses the Temperance River Gorge.

Tofte to Onion River This 2.5 mile segment connects the town of Tofte to a half mile west of Onion River, where it dead ends. There is currently no public parking available.

Grand Marais This 1.5 mile segment lies within the Grand Marais city limits. It connects to the 1-mile Grand Marais Corridor Trail that travels through the heart of the downtown area.

Grand Marais
1 mile

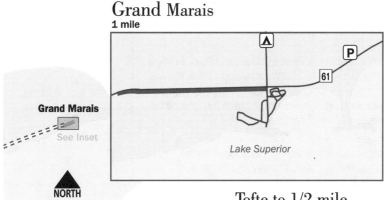

Tofte to 1/2 mile west of Onion River
2.5 miles

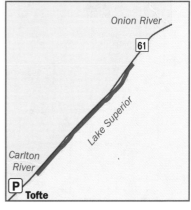

Split Rock Lighthouse State Park to Beaver Bay
8.4 miles

109

Heartland State Trail

Trail Length	50.0 miles
Surface	Asphalt, natural-groomed
Uses	Leisure bicycling, cross-country skiing, in-line skating, snowmobiling, hiking
Location & Setting	The Heartland Trail is a 50 mile multiple-use state trail constructed on an abandoned railroad line. The Trail has two segments. The East-West segment is 28 miles long and asphalt paved, running between Park Rapids Walker. The North-South segment is 22 miles long, undeveloped but mowed, and runs between Walker and just south of Cass Lake. The East West segment is mostly open area while the North-South segment is wooded and lakes.
Information	DNR Information Center 651-296-6153
Counties	Hubbard, Cass

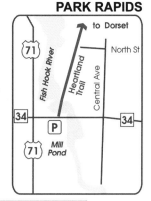

PARK RAPIDS

West Trailhead Begins in Heartland Park in Park Rapids. Going east on HWY 34 through Park Rapids, you turn north on Central Avenue (there is a sign). Turn west on North Street which leads into the park which offers excellent facilities.

Park Rapids is named for the park-like groves and prairies that existed. Parking, restrooms, water, picnic area, shelter, restaurants, and lodging available in the area.

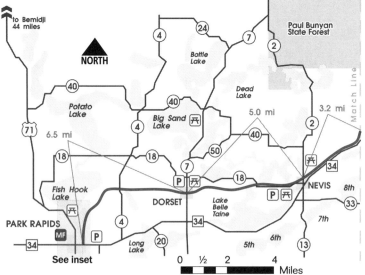

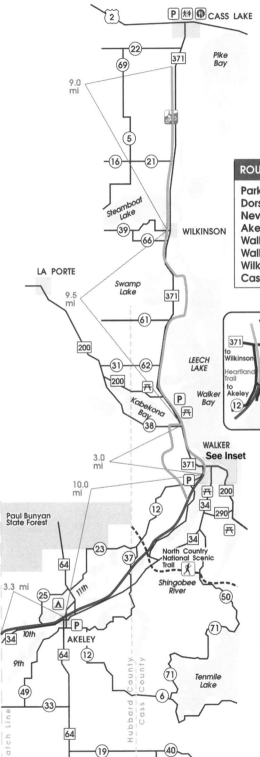

East Trail The trail ends abruptly. Ride the last quarter mile into Walker on city streets. Walker is situated on the shores of Leech Lake, one of the largest lakes in the State. You will find ample facilities in Walker.

ROUTE SLIP	INCREMENT	TOTAL
Park Rapids		
Dorset	6.5	6.5
Nevis	5.0	11.5
Akeley	6.5	17.0
Walker	10.0	28.0
Walker Bay	3.0	31.0
Wilkinson	9.5	40.5
Cass Lake	9.0	49.5

Parking, restrooms, water, picnic area, and shelter are on the north side of the trail in Akeley. One block from the trail is a huge Paul Bunyan statue at the municipal park on Main Street.

Bicycle rentals, refreshments, and restrooms are available in most communities along the trail.

111

Lake Wobegon Rail-Trail

Trail Length	28 miles
Surface	Asphalt
Uses	Leisure bicycling, hiking, in-line skating, cross-country skiing
Location & Setting	This trail, which opened in 1998, was built on old railbed and runs from Avon west to Sauk Centre. It is 28 miles long with a 10 foot wide asphalt surface. There are mile markers every half mile and warning signs before every stop sign. Parking and most facilities are accessible in each of the 5 towns along the route.
Information	Stearns County Parks 320-255-6172
County	Stearns

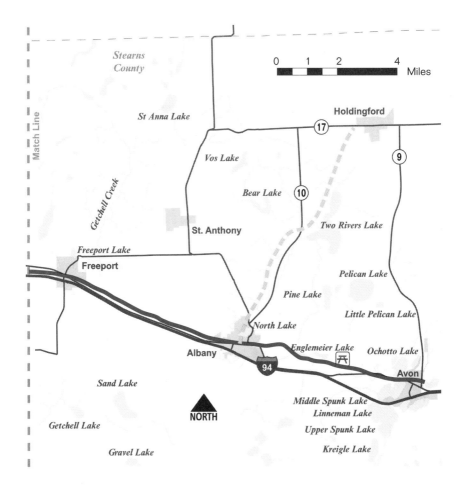

Itasca State Park

Trail Length	17.0 miles
Surface	Asphalt
Uses	Leisure bicycling, cross-country skiing, in-line skating, hiking
Location & Setting	Itasca State Park, where the Mississippi River begins, is a 32,690 acre park established in 1891. It is located 20 miles north of Park Rapids, on Hwy 71. Setting is heavily wooded plus several lakes. The 5.5 mile paved bicycle trail runs along the east side of Lake Itasca. For a extended tour of the park, continue around Wilderness Drive for another 11 miles.
Information	DNR Information Center 651-296-6157
Counties	Clearwater, Hubbard, Becker

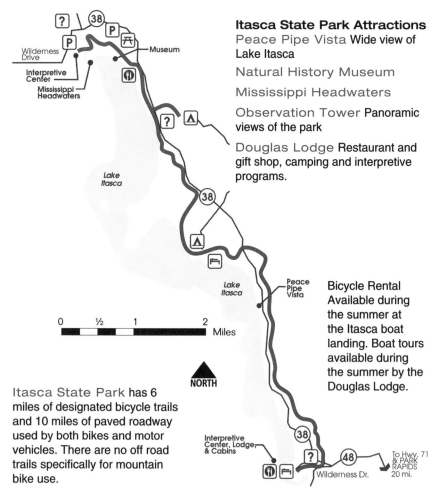

Itasca State Park Attractions

Peace Pipe Vista Wide view of Lake Itasca

Natural History Museum

Mississippi Headwaters

Observation Tower Panoramic views of the park

Douglas Lodge Restaurant and gift shop, camping and interpretive programs.

Bicycle Rental Available during the summer at the Itasca boat landing. Boat tours available during the summer by the Douglas Lodge.

Itasca State Park has 6 miles of designated bicycle trails and 10 miles of paved roadway used by both bikes and motor vehicles. There are no off road trails specifically for mountain bike use.

Mesabi Trail

Trail Length	132.0 miles (when completed)
Surface	Asphalt
Uses	Leisure bicycling, hiking, in-line skating
Location & Setting	Some 66 miles of this planned 132 mile trail between Grand Rapids and Ely are completed and asphalt paved. The longest paved sections run from Grand Rapids to Taconite for 13 miles; from Nashwauk east to Kinney for 30 miles; and from Mt. Iron to Eveleth for 13 miles. The trail is partially built on old railbed and is 10 to 14 feet wide. Most services are available at the communities in route.
Information	Mesabi Trail 218-254-0086
Counties	St. Louis, Lake

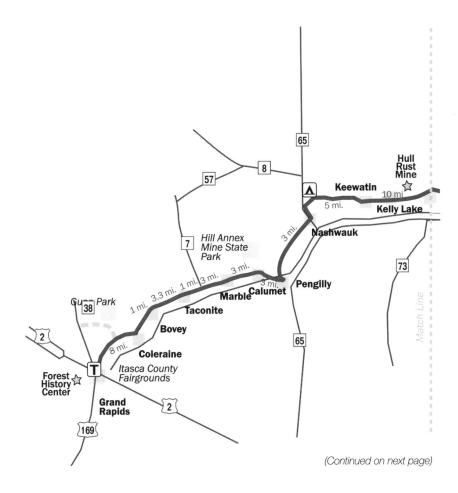

(Continued on next page)

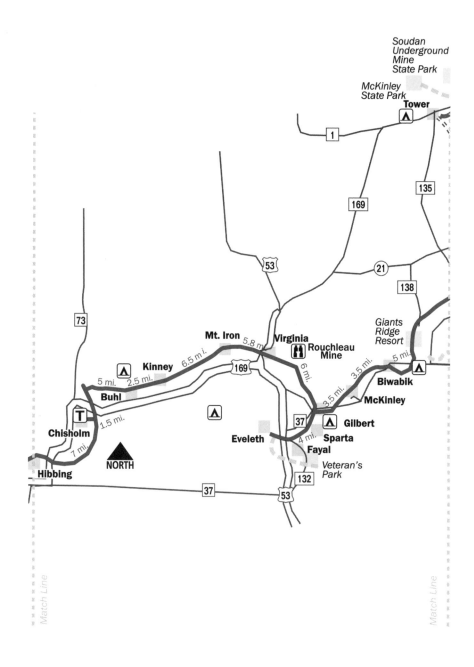

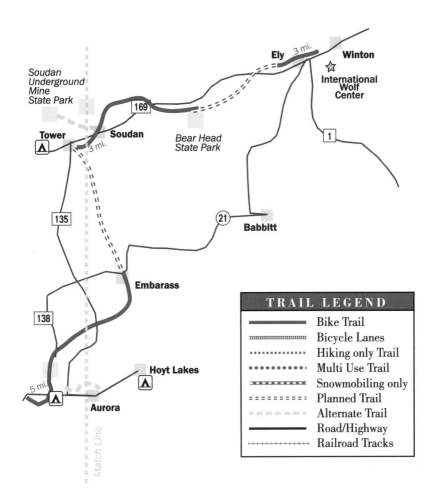

Soudan
Underground
Mine
State Park

Tower

Soudan

Bear Head
State Park

3 mi.

169

Ely   3 mi.

Winton

International
Wolf
Center

1

135

21

Babbitt

Embarass

138

Hoyt Lakes

5 mi.

Aurora

Match Line

TRAIL LEGEND	
━━━━━	Bike Trail
▥▥▥▥▥	Bicycle Lanes
··············	Hiking only Trail
●●●●●●	Multi Use Trail
▬▪▬▪▬▪	Snowmobiling only
= = = = = = = =	Planned Trail
▥ ▥ ▥ ▥ ▥ ▥	Alternate Trail
━━━━━	Road/Highway
┼┼┼┼┼┼┼┼┼	Railroad Tracks

Mi-Gi-Zi Trail

Trail Length	19.0 miles
Surface	Asphalt – 8 to10 feet wide
Uses	Leisure bicycling, cross-county skiing, in-line skating, hiking
Location & Setting	The Mi-Gi-Zi Trail winds around the Pike Bay and the east side of Cass Lake through big red pines in north central Minnesota's Chippewa National Forest. You can access the trail from the Forest Supervisor's Office in Cass Lake, across from Cass Lake Wayside Rest on Hwy 2, Norway Beach Recreation Area off Hwy 2, or South Pike Bay Picnic Area on the Pike Bay Loop road. A popular starting point is the Norway Beach campgrounds in the summer. This beautiful trail is named for the bald eagle, migizi in Ojibwe language.
Information	Chippewa National Forest 219-335-8632
County	Hubbard

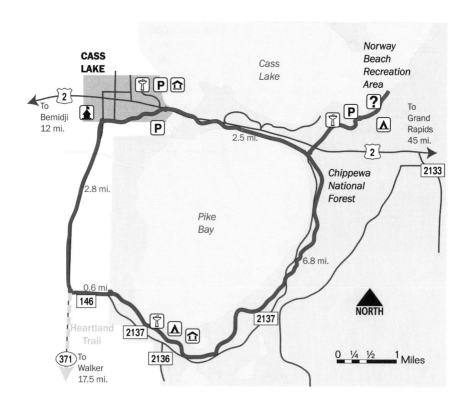

Mississippi River County Park

Trail Length	2.5 miles
Surface	Crushed stone
Uses	Leisure bicycling, hiking, cross-country skiing
Location & Setting	This County Park has 2.5 miles of year round trails. It's located about 6 miles north of Sartell and 10 miles north of St. Cloud. The setting is woods, prairies and open area. Facilities include toilets, shelters, picnic areas and a boat launch.
Information	Stearns County Parks 320-255-6172
Counties	Stearns

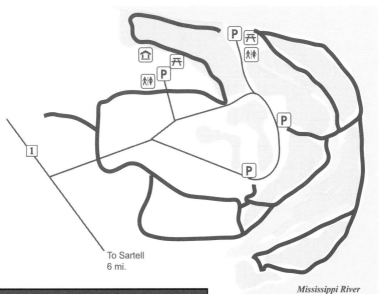

To Sartell
6 mi.

Mississippi River

SYMBOL LEGEND

🏖	Beach/Swimming	**MF**	Multi-Facilities
🚲	Bicycle Repair	**P**	Parking
🏠	Cabin	🛉	Picnic
▲	Camping	🔺	Ranger Station
🛶	Canoe Launch	🚻	Restrooms
+	First Aid	🏠	Shelter
🍴	Food	**T**	Trailhead
GC	Golf Course	🏛	Visitor Center
?	Information	💧	Water
🛏	Lodging	🔭	Overlook/ Observation

Paul Bunyon State Trail

Trail Length	100 miles
Surface	see chart below
Uses	Leisure bicycling, cross-country skiing, in-line skating, snowmobiling, hiking
Location & Setting	North central Minnesota. Primarily located on abandoned rail grade, the trail links the towns of Brainerd, Walker and Bemidji plus several other small communities in route. It is generally level. The setting consists of woods lakes, & open country.
Information	Minnesota Department of Natural Resources 218-755-2265
Counties	Crow Wing, Cass, Hubbard, Beltrami

From	Surface	Width	Length	Map Symbol
Brainerd/Baxter to Hackensack	asphalt	10 ft wide	48.5 miles	A
Lake Bemidji to Mississippi River	asphalt	12 ft wide	5.3 miles	A
Walker to Hubard/Beltrami County line	ballast*	10 ft wide	28.0 miles	B
Hubbard/Betrami County line to Bemidji	ballast*	10 ft wide	18.0 miles	B

asphalt planned

Mileage Guide

	Increments	Totals	
Baxter			100.0
Merrifield	9.0	9.0	91.0
Nisswa	5.8	14.8	85.2
Pequot Lakes	6.2	21.0	79.0
Jenkins	3.0	24.0	76.0
Pine River	6.0	30.0	70.0
Backus	8.8	38.8	61.2
Elackensack	7.6	46.4	53.6
Walker	16.8	63.2	36.8
Benedict	7.8	71.0	29.0
Laporte	5.2	76.2	23.8
Guthrie	6.2	82.4	17.6
Nary	5.2	87.6	12.4
Bemidji	9.6	97.2	2.8
Lake Bemidji SP	2.8	100.0	

Crow Wing State Park
Phone: (218) 829-8022
The historic Red River Ox Cart Trail goes through the once prosperous town of Old Crow Wing. Park visitors will enjoy the natural beauty of the confluence of the Crow Wing and Mississippi Rivers. Hike the 18 mi of trails to capture a sense of the area's history. There are 6.5 miles of cross-country skitrail. Open year round from 8 am to 10 pm. Located 9 miles south of Brainerd on Hwy 371. Park headquarter is 1 mile west of 371 on Cr 27. There is a parking permit fee.

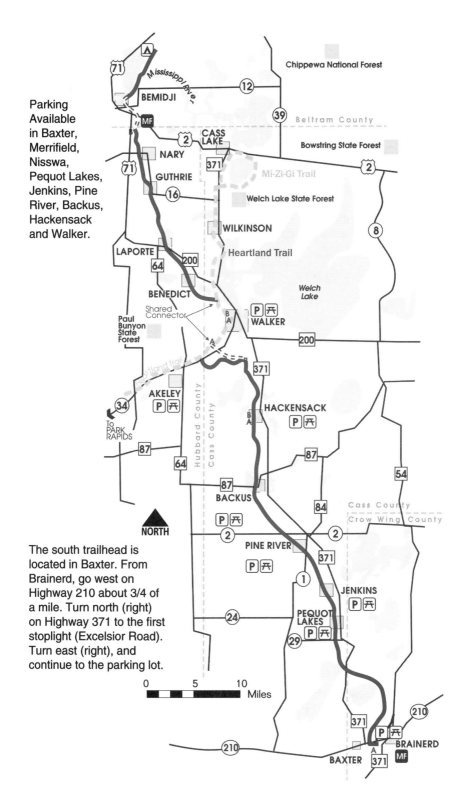

Parking Available in Baxter, Merrifield, Nisswa, Pequot Lakes, Jenkins, Pine River, Backus, Hackensack and Walker.

Chippewa National Forest

BEMIDJI

Mississippi River

Beltram County

CASS LAKE

NARY

Bowstring State Forest

GUTHRIE

Mi-Zi-Gi Trail

Welch Lake State Forest

WILKINSON

Heartland Trail

LAPORTE

BENEDICT

Welch Lake

Shared Connector

Paul Bunyon State Forest

P 🏕 WALKER

Heartland Trail

AKELEY P 🏕

To PARK RAPIDS

Hubbard County   Cass County

HACKENSACK P 🏕

BACKUS P 🏕

Cass County
Crow Wing County

PINE RIVER P 🏕

JENKINS P 🏕

PEQUOT LAKES P 🏕

NORTH

The south trailhead is located in Baxter. From Brainerd, go west on Highway 210 about 3/4 of a mile. Turn north (right) on Highway 371 to the first stoplight (Excelsior Road). Turn east (right), and continue to the parking lot.

0   5   10
Miles

BRAINERD P 🏕 MF

BAXTER

Soo Line Trail

Trail Length	11.0 miles, plus 8 miles planned
Surface	Paved, 8 feet wide
Uses	Leisure bicycling, cross-country skiing, in-line skating, hiking
Location & Setting	The 10 foot parallel path is open to A.T.V.'s and snowmobiling. The Trail extends from Onomia to Isle, south of Mill Lacs Lake, along the former Soo Line railroad grade, and passes through the village of Wahkon. It meanders through forest, farmland and wetlands.
Information	Mill Lacs Area Tourism Council 888-350-2692
County	Mill Lacs

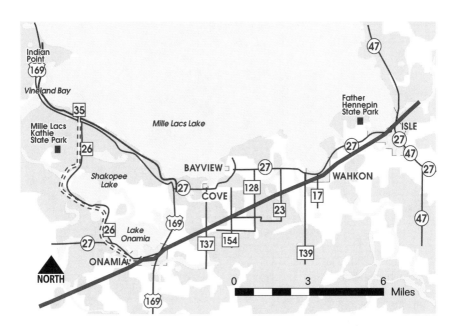

Father Hennepin State Park and Kathio State Park are both easily accessible from both ends of the trail. Father Hennepin State Park is linked via low volume city street in Isle. Kathio State Park, five miles north west of Onamia, is linked via County State Aid Highway 26 which also has a relatively low traffic volume.

The bike trail is within a duel use corridor. There is also a ten foot unpaved portion for A.T.V. users that parallels the bike trail.

Onamia has renovated a depot into a rest stop along the trail. There is an exhibit, the 'Ellen Ruth" a former Mille Lacs Lake Launch, which is only one block from the trail.

St. Croix State Park

Trail Length	6.0 miles
Surface	Paved
Uses	Leisure bicycling, cross-country skiing, in-line skating, hiking
Location & Setting	St. Croix State Park borders the St. Croix River and Wisconsin state line and is located approximately 60 miles north of the Twin Cities and 15 miles east of Hinckley. It is the largest state park in Minnesota with over 33,000 acres of forest, meadows and streams.
Information	St. Croix State Park 320-384-6591
County	Pine

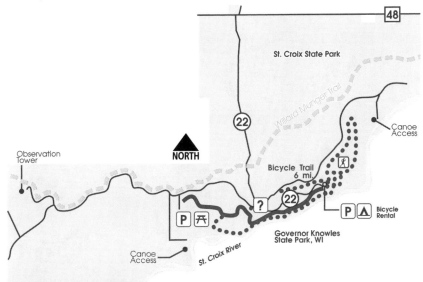

St. Croix State Park Visitor Facilities
- Six miles of surfaced bicycle trails
- Bicycle and canoe rental
- Campsites and showers
- Guesthouse
- Canoe campsites and landings
- Souvenir shop with limited groceries
- Ice and wood sales
- 127 miles of foot trails
- 21 miles of ski trails
- 80 miles of groomed & marked snowmobile trails
- Forestry towers and scenic overlooks

Taconite Trail

Trail Length	165 miles (6 miles paved)
Surface	Paved, undeveloped
Uses	Leisure bicycling, hiking, in-line skating, cross-country skiing
Location & Setting	A 165 mile trail located between Grand Rapids and Ely, of which the first 6 miles out of Grand Rapids is paved. The remaining surface is undeveloped, and is used primarily for snowmobiling.
Information	Dept. of Natural Resources Information Ctr. 651-296-6157
Counties	St. Louis, Itasca

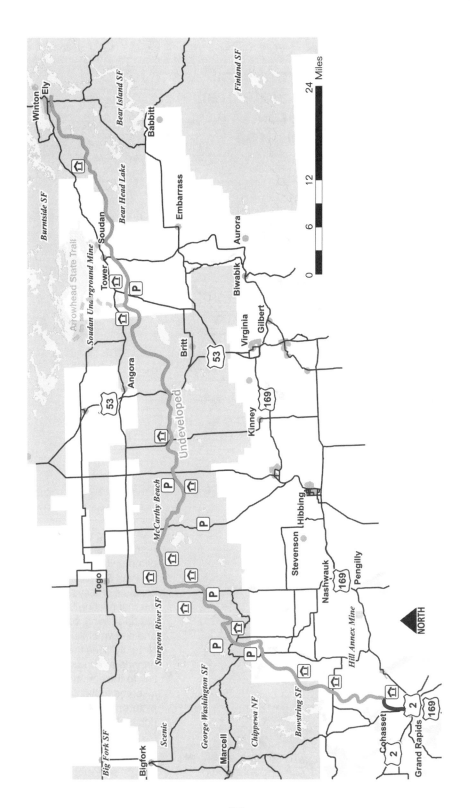

Willard Munger State Trail System

Western Waterfront Trail
Willard Munger State Trail
Sunrise Prairie Trail
Hardwood Creek Trail
Gateway Trail
Alex Laveau Trail

(East Metro Section)

The Willard Munger Trail is the longest paved trail in the country and the greatest recreation resource in the state of Minnesota.

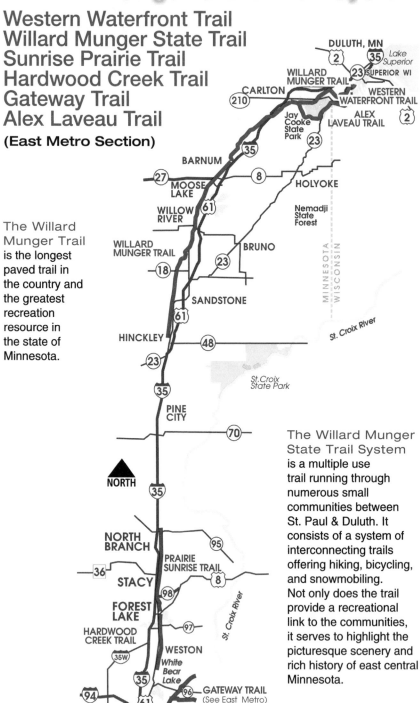

The Willard Munger State Trail System is a multiple use trail running through numerous small communities between St. Paul & Duluth. It consists of a system of interconnecting trails offering hiking, bicycling, and snowmobiling. Not only does the trail provide a recreational link to the communities, it serves to highlight the picturesque scenery and rich history of east central Minnesota.

Western Waterfront Trail

Trail Length	5.0 miles
Surface	Paved for about a mile; rest is screenings
Uses	Leisure bicycling, hiking
Location & Setting	Located south of Duluth proper, bordering the west side of Spirit Lake and the St. Louis River and across the Street from the Lake Superior Zoo. It connects to the Willard Munger Trail at its north trailhead and Commonwealth Avenue at its south trailhead.
Information	Duluth Parks & Recreation Dept 218-723-3612
Counties	Carlton

Alex Laveau Trail

Trail Length	16 miles, including 10 miles of designated shoulder
Surface	Asphalt: 6 miles plus paved shoulder
Uses	Leisure bicycling, cross-country skiing, in-line skating, hiking
Location & Setting	From Carlton southeast through Wrenshall to Hwy. 23. North on Hwy. 23, along a designated shoulder to Hwy. 105 south of Duluth.
Information	Munger Trail Towns Association 218-485-5410
Counties	Carlton, St. Louis

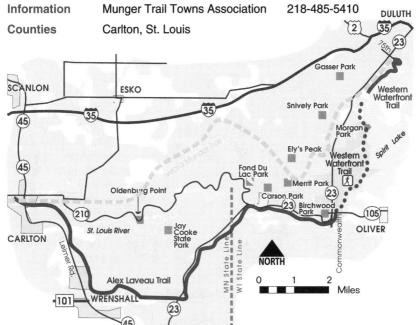

Duluth Area Attractions

Lakewalk A mile plus boardwalk and bicycle trail from Canal Park to 26th Avenue E. along the lake shore.

Fitger's Brewery Complex Shops and restaurants along the lake shore with bike and carriage paths.

The Depot 506 W. Michigan St. Houses 3 museums, visual arts, and 4 performing groups.

Marine Museum and Canal Park Visitor Center Interpretive geologic and maritime exhibits.

Hinckley Area Attractions

Hinckley Fire Museum Features logging and railroad exhibits, and the restored Depot Agent's office and living quarters.

Hinckley Flea Market Highway 48 East, Midwest's largest indoor/outdoor Flea Market.

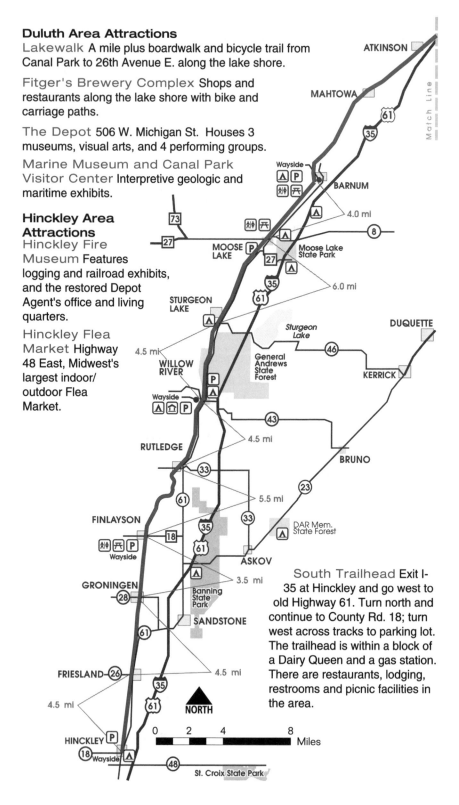

South Trailhead Exit I-35 at Hinckley and go west to old Highway 61. Turn north and continue to County Rd. 18; turn west across tracks to parking lot. The trailhead is within a block of a Dairy Queen and a gas station. There are restaurants, lodging, restrooms and picnic facilities in the area.

Willard Munger State Trail

Trail Length	76.0 miles (including 3 planned miles)
Surface	Asphalt
Uses	Leisure bicycling, cross-country skiing, in-line skating, snowmobiling, hiking
Location & Setting	The trail currently extends from Hinckley to Duluth, but will eventually run all the way from St. Paul to Duluth through a series of interconnecting trails. The trail is laid on an old railbed, asphalt surface, and largely flat with scattered forest, trees, and considerable farmland. The sections from Carlton to Duluth provides views of the St. Louis River, forest area, and rock cuts.
Information	Munger Trail Town Association 888-263-0586
Counties	Pine, Carlton

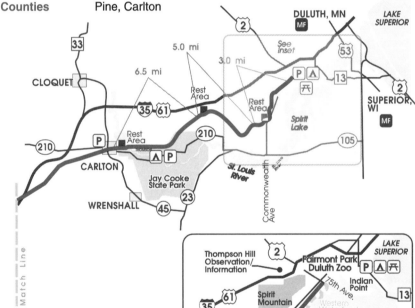

North Trailhead On Grand Ave., Highway 23, across from the zoo at 75th Avenue. Parking, picnic area with restaurants and lodging nearby. There is a municipal campground at Indian Point within a quarter mile of the trail and on the St. Louis River.

Sunrise Prairie Trail

Trail Length	15.0 miles: 10 feet wide plus parallel dirt path
Surface	Paved
Uses	Leisure bicycling, cross-country skiing, in-line skating, hiking
Location & Setting	The trail is located in Chicago County and runs from just north of Forest Lake to North Branch. It continues parallel to Highway 61.
Information	Chisago County Parks Dept. 651-674-2345
County	Chisago

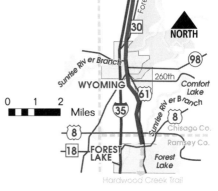

Hardwood Creek Trail

Trail Length	9.5 miles
Surface	Paved
Uses	Leisure bicycling, cross-country skiing, in-line skating, hiking
Location & Setting	The trail is located in Washington County and runs between Hugo and Forest Lake. It closely parallels Highway 61.
Information	Hardwood Creek Regional Trail 651-430-8370
County	Washington

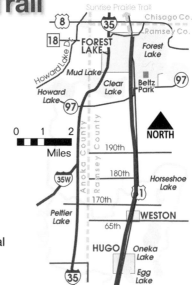

Mountain Bicycling Opportunities

Battle Creek Regional Park

Trail Length   7.0 miles

Surface   Natural

Location & Setting Here you'll find varied terrain with single-track sections that branch off ski-trails requiring skill and climbing prowess. Effort level is moderate. Winds through open fields and hardwood forests. From south St. Paul, north on I-494, exiting on Valley Creek Rd eastbound. Continue for a half mile to Winthrop Street. Parking on left side of the street.

County   Ramsey

Big Aspen Trail

Trail Length   20.0 miles

Surface   Hardpack dirt & Grass

Location & Setting Big Aspen is located in the Superior NF. An 8.5 mile encompassing loop with many smaller loops. The setting is a large treadway that passes through forest on logging roads and old railroad grades. There are several scenic vistas, making this trail especially popular. From Virginia, take Hwy 53 north for 8 miles to CR302, then north for 1 mile to CR405. North on 405 for 2 miles to the parking lot.

County   St. Louis

Bronk Unit (R. Dorer SF)

Trail Length   7.5 miles

Surface   Packed dirt

Location & Setting The trail consists of two narrow loops, which follow the edge of the woods as they go around the ridge. Off the north loop are spur trails, which go to the scenic overlooks of the Stockton and Mississippi River Valleys. From Stockton, north 2.1 miles to Hillsdale Township Rd. #6, then east 1.2 miles to the upper parking lot. Trailhead is around gate to the right.

County   Winona

Cascade Trail

Trail Length   18.0 miles

Surface   Harkpack ski trail, paved & gravel road

Location & Setting Ride starts out flat, then becomes a long climb with an elevation variance of 850 feet. There are some swampy sections, and insects can be a problem. From Tofte, northeast 16.5 miles into the Cascade Falls parking area on US 61.

County   Cook

Cut Lake

Trail Length   10.0 miles

Surface   Logging roads, old ski trails

Location & Setting Effort level is easy to moderate. Located in the Foot Hills SF. The trails are marked for mountain biking and there is a map at the trailhead. From Pine River, west on CR 2 for 11 miles. Entrance is on the north side.

County   Cass

Deep Portage Trail

Trail Length   11.0 miles

Surface   Natural, mowed

Location & Setting The setting is wooded and rolling. The effort level ranges from easy to difficult. Take CR 5 east of Hackensack to Woodrow Twp Rd, south to Rte 46, then east to the entrance. Parking and trailhead is by the Interpretive Center at the end of the service road.

County   Cass

Eliason Tower Trail

Trail Length	12.0 miles
Surface	Gravel & grassy logging roads
Location & Setting	The west leg of the trail is a steep, 300 foot climb or descent. The east and north legs are easy and gently rolling. The south leg involves some stream crossings. Some great views of Lake Superior. No facilities along the route. From Grand Marais, northeast on Hwy 61 for 8 miles to CR 14, then north for 3 miles to the pull-off where the road makes a sharp turn to the east and you can park.
	County Cook

French Rapids Trail

Trail Length	7.5 miles
Surface	Grass & dirt
Location & Setting	The terrain around this trail is hilly and wooded. There are sandy sections and steep climbs. The trail is not well marked. Effort level is moderate to difficult. From Brainerd northeast on Hwy 210 to airport exit (Rte 142), then left for 2.4 miles to an unmarked road. Turn left and follow to the dead end, which is the trailhead.
	County Crow Wing

Gegoka Flathorn

Trail Length	20.0 miles
Surface	Natural
Location & Setting	Effort level is moderate. Gegoka Flathorn is located in the Superior NF. Large loops with several optional trails. The setting consists of woods, wetlands, lakes, ponds, with rolling forest roads and some rocky hills. Forests are largely pine, birch aspen, and maple. From Isabella, Hwy 1 west about 6 miles to Gegoka Beach Lodge. Isabella is 60 miles north of Duluth on Hwy 1.
	County Lake

Giants Ridge Trail

Trail Length	21.5 miles
Surface	Ski Trails

Location & Setting Consists of 3 trails: Laurentian - 5.5 miles, easy to moderate; Silver, 6 miles, moderate to difficult; Wynne Lake Overlook - 10 miles, moderate. Well maintained ski trails. Setting varies from rolling terrain, woods to lake areas. From Biwabik east on Hwy 135 to CR 138, then north 3 miles to the entrance.

County St. Louis

Gooseberry Falls State Park

Trail Length	12.0 miles
Surface	Grassy singletrack

Location & Setting The setting for this state park includes forest, the Lake Superior shoreline, five waterfalls, and the Gooseberry River. There are many interconnecting loops. Wildlife is common. From Two Harbors, 13 miles northeast on Hwy 61, or about 35 miles north of Duluth.

County Lake

Hayes Lake State Park

Trail Length	5.0 miles
Surface	Natural

Location & Setting Hayes Lake State Park offers hundreds of square miles of untamed landscape. The central focus to the park is the lake and north fork of the Roseau River. The topography is essentially flat with beach ridges and river valleys. The park is located 22 miles southeast or Roseau, off Hwy 4. The mountain bike trail starts at Hayes Dam

County Roseau

Hidden Valley/Trezona Trail

Trail Length   13.0 miles

Surface   Gravel roads, grassy ski trail

Location & Setting Effort level is moderate. Multiple loops, some steep descents, and scenic views. From Ely, Central Ave north for 2 blocks. Use parking lot behind the Wilderness Outfitters store.

County   St. Louis

Holzinger Lodge Trail

Trail Length   5.0 miles

Surface   Grass, hardpack, roots

Location & Setting The lower 2.5 mile loop of this trail is an 8-foot wide ski trail with a moderate effort level. The upper 2.5 mile loop is challenging and single track with a 380-foot elevation gain. All services are available in Winona. From Winona, exit Hwy 14/61 at Huff St. southbound. Right on Lake Blvd. for 0.7 miles, then west to Holzinger Lodge.

County   Winona

Jay Cooke State Park

Trail Length   12.0 miles

Surface   Grass, rocks, paved

Location & Setting Jay Cooke State Park consists of massive rock formations, hardwoods forests, steep valleys, with beautiful views of the St. Louis River. The park offers picnic area, camping, and shelter. Trails are well maintained. Effort level is moderate. From Duluth, west on I-35W to Hwy 210, then east for 5 miles to park entrance.

County   Carlton

Kruger Unit (R. Dover SF)

Trail Length   8.5 miles

Surface   Natural

Location & Setting   Trail is mostly double-track and rugged, over bluffs and traversing the valley of the Zumbro River. Difficulty is moderate to difficult. Located in the R. Dorer SF. From Wabasha, west on Hwy 60 to CR 81, then south for 2.5 miles past the campground to the small dirt road past the ranger station.

County   Wabasha

Lake Bemidji State Park

Trail Length   9.0 miles

Surface   Grassy

Location & Setting   Surface is rolling topography with swamps and bogs, pine-moraine. Located on the north shore of Lake Bemidji, the forest is a mixture of state pine, jack pine barrens, birch, tamarack-spruce, oaks, basswood, and hard maple. From Bemidji 5 miles north and 1.7 miles east on CR 21 to park entrance.

County   Crow Wing

Lake Bronson State Park

Trail Length   5.0 miles

Surface   Natural

Location & Setting   The Park is located in the northwest corner of Minnesota. It sits between the prairie of the Red River Valley to the west, and rolling hills of forest to the east. The trail surface is natural, and consists of a 3 mile loop and a 2 mile spur. Access to the park is from Hwy 28.

County   Kittson

Lake Elmo Park Reserve

Trail Length	8.0 miles
Surface	Grassy doubletrack, hardpack singletrack

Location & Setting Effort level is easy to moderate. Rolling terrain. From I-94, north on Keats Avenue for a mile to the entrance. Parking is a mile further on the left.

County Ramsey

Land O'Lakes State Forest

Trail Length	15.0 miles
Surface	Mowed grass, dirt

Location & Setting The setting is rolling hills, forest, lakes, and small ponds. There are numerous resorts, cabins, and private campgrounds in the forest boundary. From Outing, north on Hwy 6 to CR 48, then west 1 mile to the trailhead.

County Cass

Lawrence Unit (part of MN Valley State RA)

Trail Length	13.5 miles
Surface	Grass, dirt

Location & Setting Setting consists of wetlands, wooded areas, prairie, and savanna uplands. There are several plank bridges over marshy areas. Abundant wildlife. There is an entrance fee.

County Scott

Maplelag Trails

Trail Length   6.5 miles

Surface   Natural

Location & Setting Trail sets on private land and is well maintained with moderate grades. Designed for cross-county skiing. Food, and lodging are available at Maplelag. From Callaway, go a 1/2 mile north on Hwy 59 to CR 14. East for 3 miles, then north on CR 23 for 1.7 miles. East on CR 110 (Goat Ranch Rd.) for 3.5 miles to the entrance on the south side of the road.

County   Becker

McCarthy Beach State Park

Trail Length   15.5 miles

Surface   Grassy, single and double track

Location & Setting The Park is in a deeply wooded area with rolling hills and small valleys, located between two major lakes - Sturgeon Lake and Side Lake. The trails follow the ridge tops of the park's moraines. From Hibbing north on Hwy 169 to CR 5, then north 15 miles to the park entrance.

County   St. Louis

Mount Kato Mountain Bike Park

Trail Length   7.0 miles

Surface   Natural

Location & Setting Trail is mostly single-track. Effort level ranges from easy to difficult. Opened in 1996, Mount Kato's main loop, beautiful and challenging, with three climbs, and mainly moderate. From Mankato, take Hwy 169 south to Hwy 66, then south on Hwy 66 for 1 mile to the Mount Kato Ski & Bike complex.

County   Blue Earth

Movil Maze

Trail Length	6.5 miles
Surface	Singletrack, grassy ski trails

Location & Setting Effort level is moderate to difficult. It is easy to get lost in the deep forest so bring a map. The ski trails are identified with blue diamond markers. From Bemidji, northeast on Hwy 71 for 8 miles, then north on Wildwood Road for another mile.

County Beltrami

Myre Big Island State Park

Trail Length	7.0 miles
Surface	Grassy

Location & Setting The Park offers rolling hills, shallow lakes, and marshes. Albert Lea Lake borders the park on the east. Located 3 miles southeast of Albert Lea. Take Exit 11 off I-35 and follow signs. Hwy 90 & I-35 intersect just north of Albert Lea.

County Freebom

Pancore Trail

Trail Length	16.5 miles
Surface	Old roadbed, sand, grass

Location & Setting Terrain is flat to rolling. Located in the Superior National Forest. Area is generally well signed. From Tofte at Hwy 61, north 11.5 miles on CR 2 (Sawbill Trail) to the junction of FR338.

County St. Louis

Paul Bunyan State Forest

Trail Length   10.0 miles

Surface   Dirt & forest roads

Location & Setting   The setting is forest, ponds, bogs, and some marshy areas. There are three non-connecting loop trails. These trails are not marked, and are both single and double track. Effort level is moderate to difficult. There are no designated parking facilities. Many of the forest roads are still active. From Akeley, 10 miles north on Hwy 64 to FR 2, then left to Refuge Road and Beaver Lakes Trails, one of the three loop trails.

County   Hubbard

Pillsbury State Forest

Trail Length   27.0 miles

Surface   Grassy & dirt

Location & Setting   The terrain is rolling to hilly with numerous small ponds and lakes. Effort level is moderate to difficult. Stands of maple, oak, ash, and basswood cover much of the forest. The trails are marked. From Brainerd, north and then west on CR 77 for about 10 miles. Turn southwest on Pillager FR for 2 miles. Trailhead is on the West side of road.

County   Crow Wing

Pincushion Mountain

Trail Length   15.0 miles

Surface   Grassy, dirt

Location & Setting   The setting consists of forest, lowlands, bluffs, and several footbridges. Trail is single-track loops. Effort level is moderate. Pincushion Mountain offers a spectacular overview of Lake Superior and the Superior NF. From Grand Marais, go 2 miles north on CR 12. Grand Marais is about 130 miles northeast of Duluth on Hwy 61.

County   Cook

Reno Unit (R. Dorer SF)

Trail Length	13.0 miles
Surface	Natural, road

Location & Setting The Reno Unit is part of the Richard Dorer SF. The trail is narrow two-track with some dirt road. Effort level is difficult. Beautiful scenic vistas, with deep valleys and steep ridges overlooking the Mississippi River. From LaCrescent, 17 miles south on Hwy 26 to Reno. Follow the gravel road for a mile to the parking area.

County Houston

Savanna Portage State Park

Trail Length	12.0 miles
Surface	Grass, dirt roads, single track.

Location & Setting Setting is rolling hills, lakes, bogs, and woods. Effort level is easy. The Savanna Portage was a vital link between Lake Superior and the Upper Mississippi. The rolling hills and sandy soil are remnants of past glaciers. From McGregor, take CR 14/36 northeast for 17 miles to the park entrance, then follow the gravel park road north to the Historical Marker parking area.

County Aitkin

Scenic State Park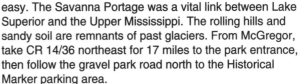

Trail Length	18.0 miles
Surface	Single & doubletrack

Location & Setting Maintained ski & hiking trails. Effort level is easy to moderate. The Park consists of rolling terrain, flat areas, and woods, encompassing Coon and Sandwich Lakes, and parts of several other lakes. From Bigfork, take County Road 7 south and then east a total of 7 miles to the park entrance.

County Itasca

Simpson Creek

Trail Length	14.0 miles
Surface	Singletrack

Location & Setting Effort level is moderate and seldom cycled. Gently rolling terrain through red and white pines, along marshes, and up glacial eskers. From Deer River northwest NW Hwy. 46 to parking at the Cutfoot Sioux Visitor Center.

County   Itasca

Snake Creek Unit (R. Doyer SF)

Trail Length	13.5 miles
Surface	Grass and hardpack

Location & Setting Snake Creek runs through a valley and the topography is rough with slopes rising 300 feet on either side of the valley floor. Effort level is moderate. Climbs follow reasonable grades. The area is forested with oak, pine, and walnut. Trails are well maintained, but watch for fallen branches and washout ruts. From Kellogg, go 4 miles south on Hwy. 61. Follow the signs. Enter the access road, but continue straight on the field road, to the Snake Creek X-C ski area.

County   Wabasha

Split Rock Lighthouse State Park

Trail Length	8.0 miles
Surface	Grass & gravel

Location & Setting The setting for this state park is the rugged Lake Superior shoreline. Trail course varies from woods, open flat country to bumpy, loose rock and steeply pitched areas. Effort level is moderate. The Split Rock Lighthouse is said to be the most photographed lighthouse in the world. There is a history center with a theatre featuring a history film of the lighthouse. Located on Hwy. 61, 20 miles northeast of Two Harbors and about 45 miles from Duluth.

County   Lake

St. Croix State Forest

Trail Length	18.0 miles
Surface	Gravel, dirt road, natural

Location & Setting Here you'll find woods, and rolling to steep hills that are often sandy and rocky. Effort level is moderate. Well into the ride there is a scenic overlook of the St. Croix River at the edge of a small ridge. Located off Hwy 48, about 22 miles east of Hinckley.

County Pine

Sugar Hills Trail

Trail Length	12.0 miles
Surface	Grassy and hardpack, logging roads

Location & Setting Effort level is moderate to difficult. Setting is hilly, with many peaks, valleys, and ridges. There are many miles of unmarked trails. Be prepared with map as reference. From Grand Rapids south on Hwy 169 for 7 miles to CR 17, then west for 2 miles to CR 449. Continue west for another 3 miles, following signs to the parking lot at a former downhill skiing facility.

County Itasca

Timber/Frear Trail

Trail Length	30.0 miles
Surface	Gravel & unmowed old logging roads.

Location & Setting The ride includes two gradual climbs, one about 100 feet. Terrain is generally level to gently rolling. From Tofte at Hwy 61, north on CR 2 (Sawbill Trail), then west on FS166 for 6 miles to FS346. Proceed north 5.5 miles to FS170, then right for a mile to the Four Mile Lake boat landing at the junction of FS347.

County St. Louis

Trout Valley Unit (R. Dorer SF)

Trail Length	7.5 miles
Surface	Packed dirt, rocky

Location & Setting Trout valley includes steep, wooded ridges and bluffs flanking the Trout Creek. The ridge tops are open agricultural land and the slopes wooded. The trail connects the valley bottom with the ridge top, providing a scenic view of the Trout, Whitewater, and Mississippi River Valley. From Winona north on Hwy 61 to the park entrance.

County Winona

Washburn Lake Trail

Trail Length	13.0 miles
Surface	Grassy & dirt

Location & Setting Trail consists of two loops with a connector. Difficulty is easy to moderate. Rolling hills with lakes and small ponds. From Outing, go north on Rte 6 for 2 miles, then west on CR 48 for half a mile. Look for a sign on north side of road.

County Cass

Whitefish Lake

Trail Length	20.0 miles
Surface	Rocky doubletrack

Location & Setting Located in the Arrowhead Region of Cook County. The trail consists of a single large loop, and skirts several lakes, ponds, and marshes. Rolling terrain and wooded areas. Effort level is moderate. From Tofte, take FR343 north to FR166, then west to FR346. North on FR346 to FF170, then left (SW) to FR357. Proceed north on FR357 to the trailhead.

County Cook

Trail Index

Trail Index (continued)

Trail Index (continued)

City to Trail Index

City to Trail Index (continued)

City to Trail Index (continued)

City to Trail Index (continued)

POPULATION CODES		
① Up to 1,000	② 1,000 to 5,000	④ 10,000 to 50,000
	③ 5,000 to 10,000	⑤ Over 50,000

County to Trail Index

County to Trail Index (continued)

Find me a place, safe and serene,

away from the terror I see on the screen.

A place where my soul can find some peace,

away from the stress and the pressures released.

A corridor of green not far from my home

for fresh air and exercise, quiet will roam.

Summer has smells that tickle my nose

and fall has the leaves that crunch under my toes.

Beware, comes a person we pass in a while

with a wave and hello and a wide friendly smile.

Recreation trails are the place to be,

to find that safe haven of peace and serenity.

By Beverly Moore, Illinois Trails Conservancy